C000109793

Complete Mus[...]

FIFE & DRUM

By Walter Sweet

Civil War Selections • Traditional Favorites • Borrowed Tunes

Each Arrangement features

Harmony, Style Marks and Guitar Chords *and* Practical Drumbeats for Snare and Bass with All Sticking

Also included are

Streetbeats and Standard Drumbeats • All Parts Shown Together

The music is supplemented with

Histories of the Tunes and Drumbeats

Audio Contents

www.melbay.com/95483EB

1 2 3 4 5 6 7 8 9 0

Visit us on the Web at www.melbay.com — E-mail us at email@melbay.com

Acknowledgments

Susan L. Cifaldi serves as Music Librarian for the Company of Fifers and Drummers, Inc., at Ivoryton, Connecticut. She manages research data and corresponds with scholars worldwide. A fifer since 1983, she also co-edited *Benjamin Clark's Drum Book 1797.* She now lives in Ellington Connecticut, or at a fife and drum event near you. Her **Histories of the Tunes and Drumbeats** gives a long-needed scholarly perspective of traditional music for fife and drum.

Kate Van Winkle Keller is the production wizard. Thanks to Kitty, the substance of this book is presented with style. Her own publications include *Giles Gibbs, Jr., His Book for the Fife.*

Several people very kindly granted permission for their work to be published here: Bob McQuillen for **Scotty O'Neil**; Roy Watrous and Bob Ward for **Crown Point** and **Drums & Guns**; Colin Sterne and Francis Goss for **Huntington**; regarding drumbeats, George P. Carroll for **York Fusiliers**; James M. Clark for **Saint Patrick's Day in the Morning** and **East Hampton's** streetbeat; and Acton Ostling Sr. for **Sisters, 300 Years, Village Quickstep, Willie Weaver, Paddy O'Toole** and **Katy Hill,** which he collected in *Music of '76*. Many thanks to Dorence E. Smith for providing the other drumbeats. Special thanks to Ralph Sweet for raising me in the tradition.

Most important are the people who keep the tradition alive: my fellow fifers and drummers. A few of them are pictured on page 104. In Indian costume is Darlene Kelly; to the right are fireman Steve Hockman with Spot, then Jim Peret, Ralph Sweet, Ralph McComb, Ed Robert, Charlie Bennett, Dick Crosson, and Carol I. Sweet (seated). The infant is Dorothy Classen, being held by Ray Classen; clockwise are Ruth Classen, Robin Niemitz, Ed Bednarz, Rick Kelly, Walt Sweet, Sue Cifaldi, Dorence Smith, Ray King, George Yeramian, Charlie Garrow, John Kupernik and Steve Niemitz.

About the Author

Walter D. Sweet is a native Connecticut fifer with 32 years' experience. His accomplished fifing is recorded on a Compact Disc (CD), to accompany this book. He has taught fifing on all levels, and plays other instruments, too. With Yankee ingenuity, he also designs instruments: the "Waltfife" features a Boehm-style bore for traditional ease with added robustness; his Boehm flute in F above C matches the range of the fiddle for playing dance music. In real life, he is a technical writer for Jagenberg in Enfield, CT.

Previously published as The Bread and Butter of Jamming.

Contents

Complete Music for the Fife and Drum

Index at back of book. Titles in italics are drumbeats alone.

Introduction

Connecticut is one of the places where fife and drum corps do not operate in isolation: rather, they share repertoire, style, teachers, heroes, folklore, and sources of instruments and uniforms. They attend musters where they eagerly exchange all of the above. They observe unwritten ethics; they share fellowship in the fife and drum community.

These fife and drum corps are in great demand for civic events: dedications, Memorial Day services, and parades for Firemen's Carnivals. When the performance is over, members of all attending corps gather informally, often in a circle as shown on page 104. From the regional tradition, common tunes are shared in a *Jam Session*.

Without common tunes, there is no jam session. Without a jam session, musicians have no basis on which to share style, local/recent history, protocol, teamwork, or contribution to the community of fifers and drummers.

Does the communal repertoire change? Yes; gradual and regional change is natural and harmless. However, in recent years, several corps have imported whole repertoires from sources outside the region. To reject the regional repertoire is to reject the associated lore and performance practices, thereby dividing the community.

In response, I identified the region's popular fife and drum music to serve as the body of the book. The book opens with tunes which are familiar to the general public; many are suitable for Civil-War events. Some music is more popular locally than regionally. On occasion, every corps scouts new tunes for the fringes of the repertoire ("borrowed tunes"). My old corps, The Eighth Connecticut Regiment (Warehouse Point), played five such tunes. The book includes them, along with some original music.

Fifers share not only tunes, but certain performance practices, too. These practices become as much a part of fifing as the tunes themselves. Fifers in this region share an articulation pattern called "slur to staccato." The tunes are marked to capture the particulars of style local to Warehouse Point during the 1980s. The study of this style will foster skills for learning, teaching, or documenting other styles.

This book aims to serve today's fifer and drummer. Contained are 78 tunes, played at formal and informal affairs. Each tune has a harmony, based on simple chording, to enhance without overshadowing. Every tune has two sets of guitar chords: one set to accompany concert-pitch instruments, and another to accompany the popular military fife in B-flat. Each tune has a practical drumbeat in the strict Rudimental style, with fills, and all sticking. Music is traced to its 18th- and 19th-century roots. The whole is professionally presented in a single volume, with a recording on Compact Disc.

For me, fifing and drumming has many pleasures. The greatest pleasure of all is the playing of common tunes informally, and so I propose . . .

Complete Music for the Fife and Drum

Implied Understandings and Special Symbols

This page summarizes principal Rudiments (in *Italics*); it is no substitute for proper Rudimental training. *9-Stroke Rolls* may be replaced with *11-Stroke Rolls*, provided that participating drummers agree, and the sticking is natural.

Bass Sticking tends to reverse in successive measures. However, where the phrase repeats, so does the sticking. See p.3, *Battle Hymn*. Bass drumming is not mentioned at all in Bruce & Emmett. Corresponding bass parts are derived from traditional rules. According to James M. Clark, today's tradition of bass drumming developed over the last 60 years. It is not as strict as snare drumming.

Option for Streetbeats: alternate loud then soft.

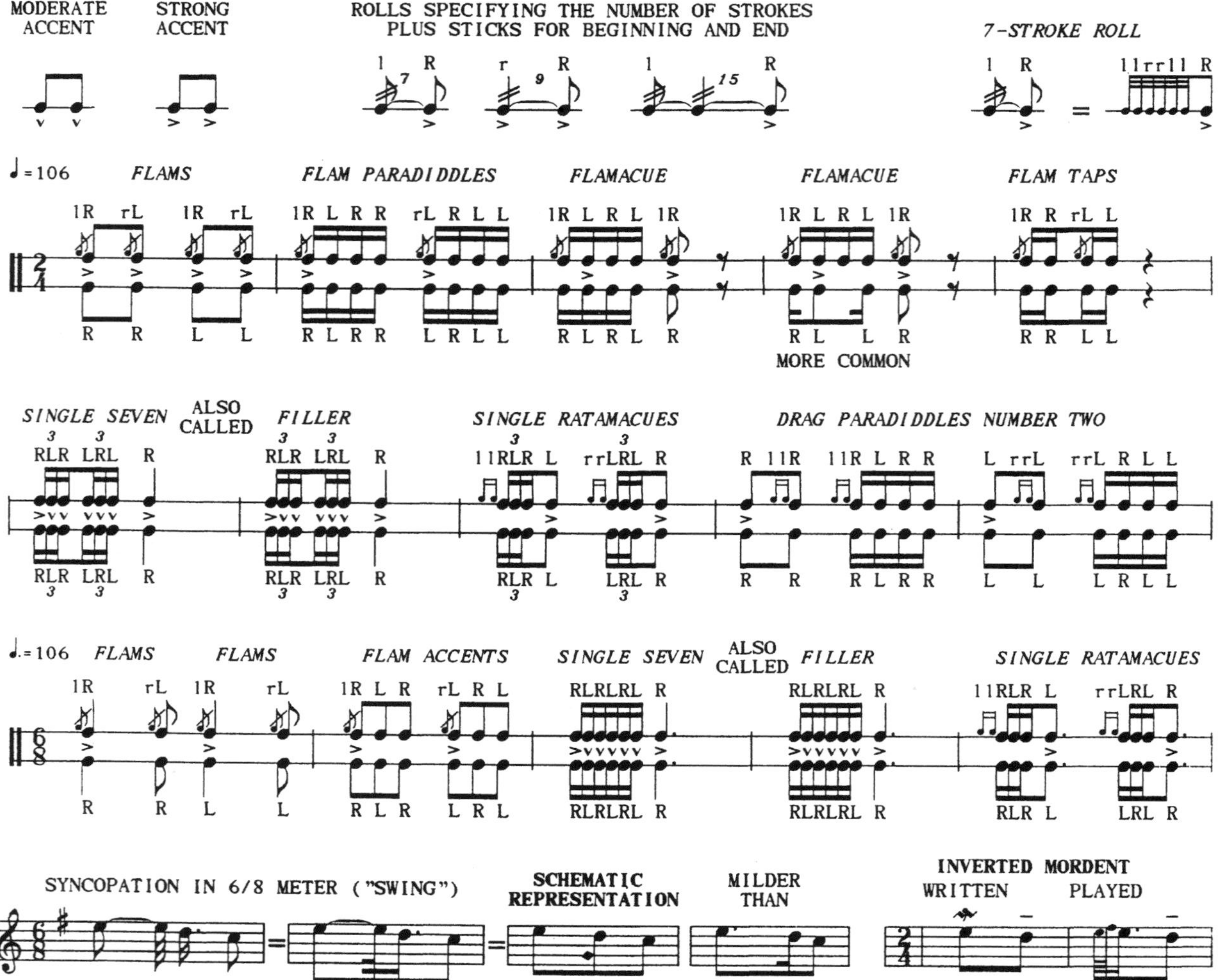

To save space, the clef and key signature are not repeated; they remain the same until superseded.

The popular military fife plays mainly in three keys. The simplest scale has the tonic with this fingering: ● ● ● ● ● ● (the fife has no low note for the pinky). The normal scale is written in D, which sounds a concert pitch of B-flat, hence the designation, B-Flat Fife. To accompany the fife, read the chords from **FIFE II.**

FIFE II is the harmony (for one fifer in six).

Compared to conventional notation, traditional fifers play one octave higher. See the fingering chart, pp.30 & 31.

Stylemarks (phrasing, syncopation, dynamics, articulation, accents and ornaments) are suggestions only.

For all Ornaments, use trill fingerings (p.31).

For the Inverted Mordent, play the main tone on the downbeat; quickly go up the scale one step then back down.

When Johnny Comes Marching Home

Glory Glory Halleluyah

The Battle Hymn of the Republic

For the drumbeat, see facing page.

4/8/21

The Battle Hymn of the Republic
Continued

Traditional

Play this phrase three times

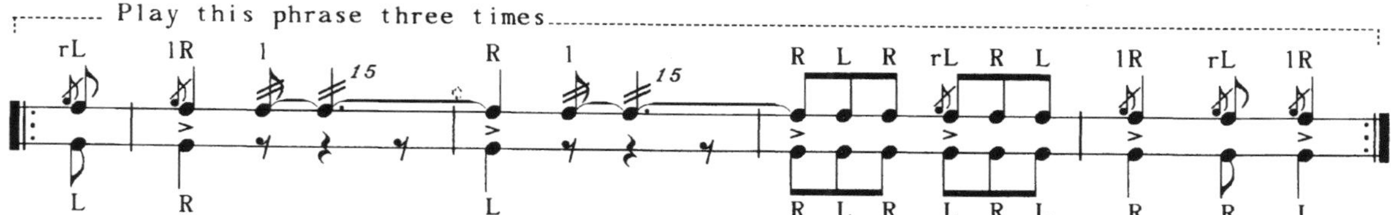

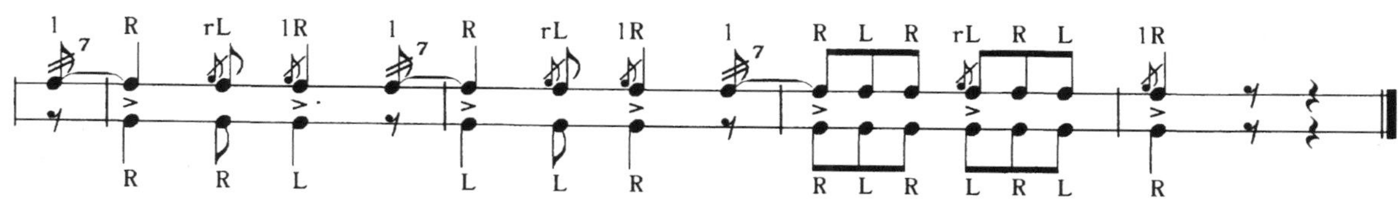

Option: Drums end the 1st strain this way for a 2nd strain in 2/4. Fifes continue in 6/8. As played by Dorence E. Smith.

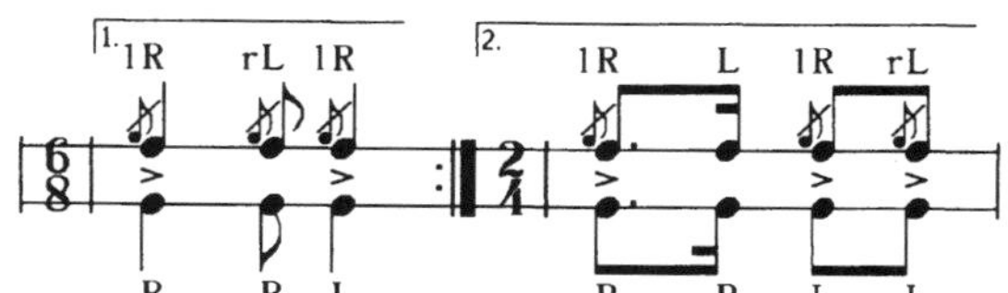

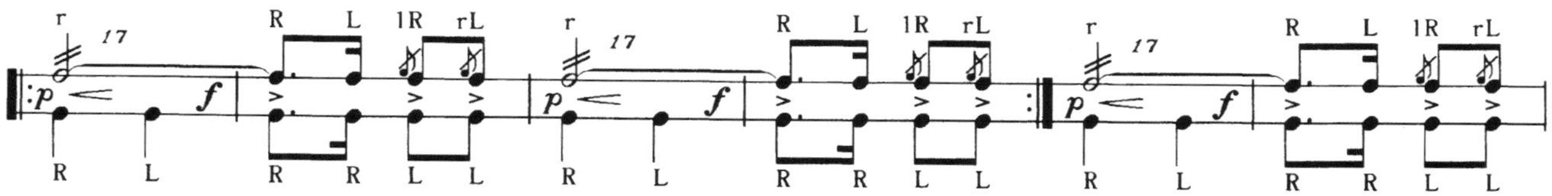

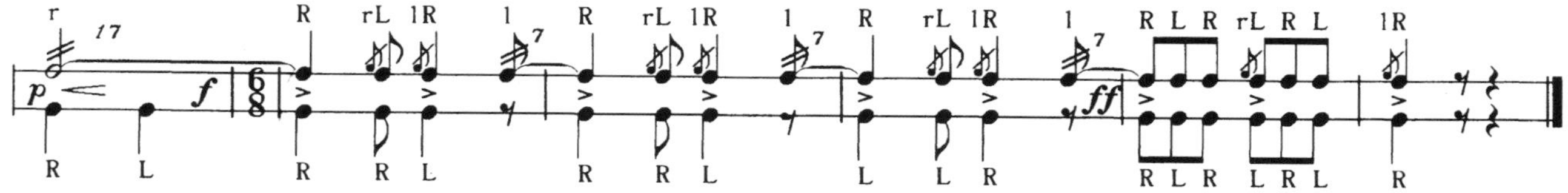

Option: 2nd time thru the tune, 1st strain, snare drummers play on the rim (the counterhoop); Basses play phrase at right:

Play 4 times

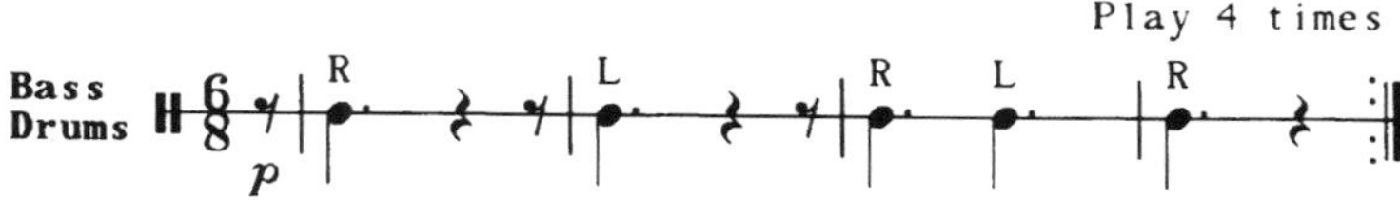

Option: Some players double the length of strains.

4/8/21

Yankee Doodle

Suggested drumbeats for both tunes: *Army Two-Four*, facing page, or *The General*, p.81.

The Frog in the Well

A general purpose drumbeat

Army Two-Four

Bruce & Emmett, 1862

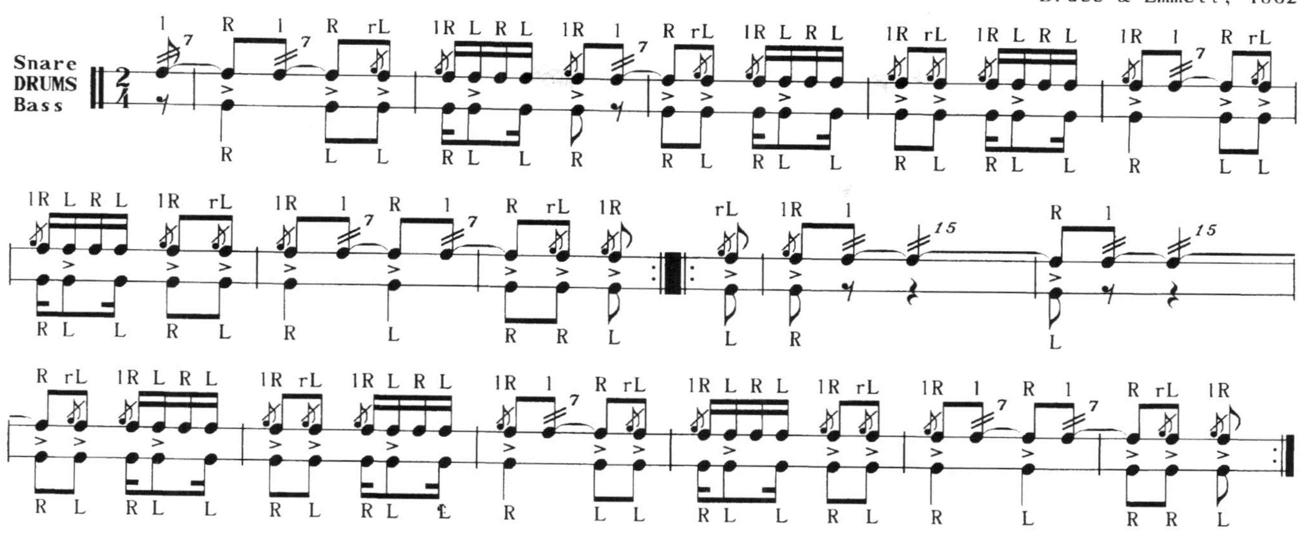

Fill

Traditional

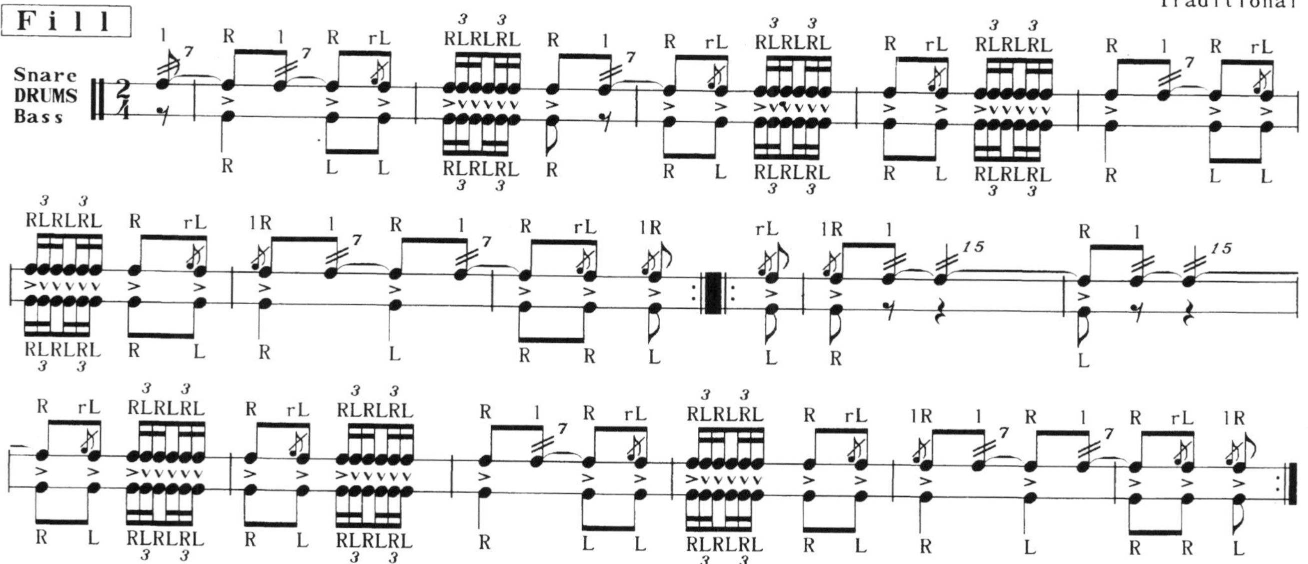

The Long March

Streetbeat

Ashworth, 1812

The Girl I Left Behind Me

Traditional

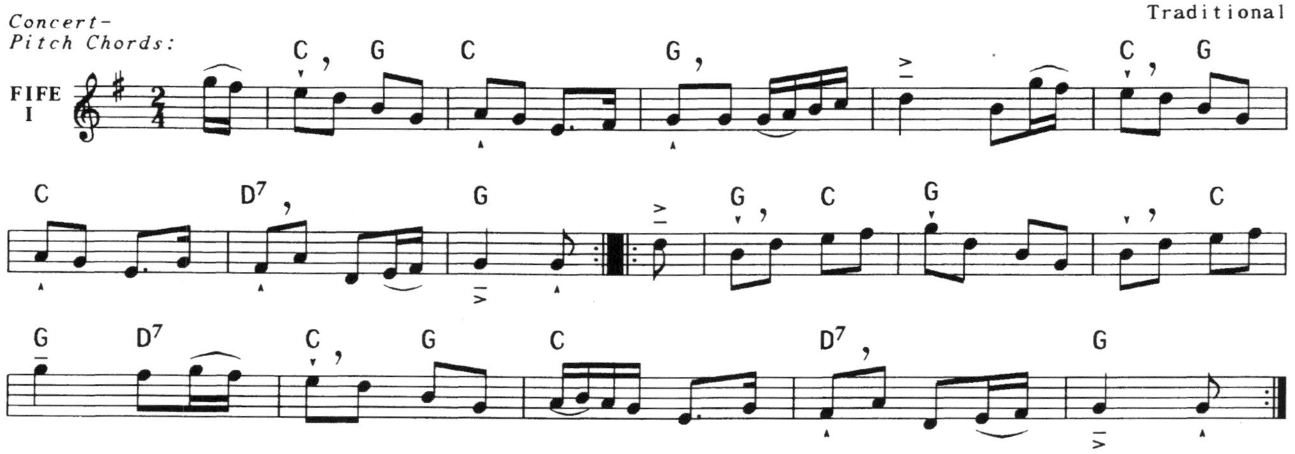
Concert-
Pitch Chords:
FIFE
I
C G C G C G
C D7 G G C G C
G D7 C G C D7 G

Walter D. Sweet

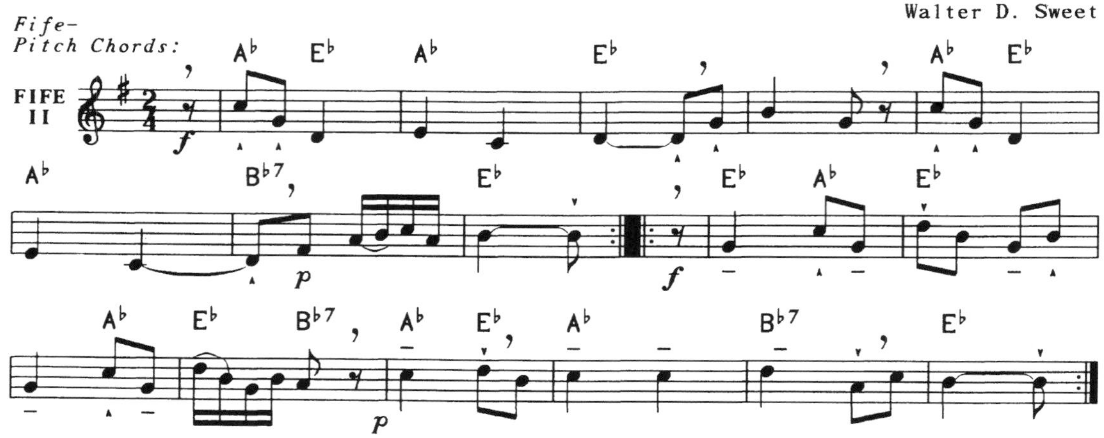
Fife-
Pitch Chords:
FIFE
II
A♭ E♭ A♭ E♭ A♭ E♭
A♭ B♭7 E♭ E♭ A♭ E♭
A♭ E♭ B♭7 A♭ E♭ A♭ B♭7 E♭

Bruce & Emmett, 1862

Snare
DRUMS
Bass

*One way to play ♪ is to click your own sticks together.

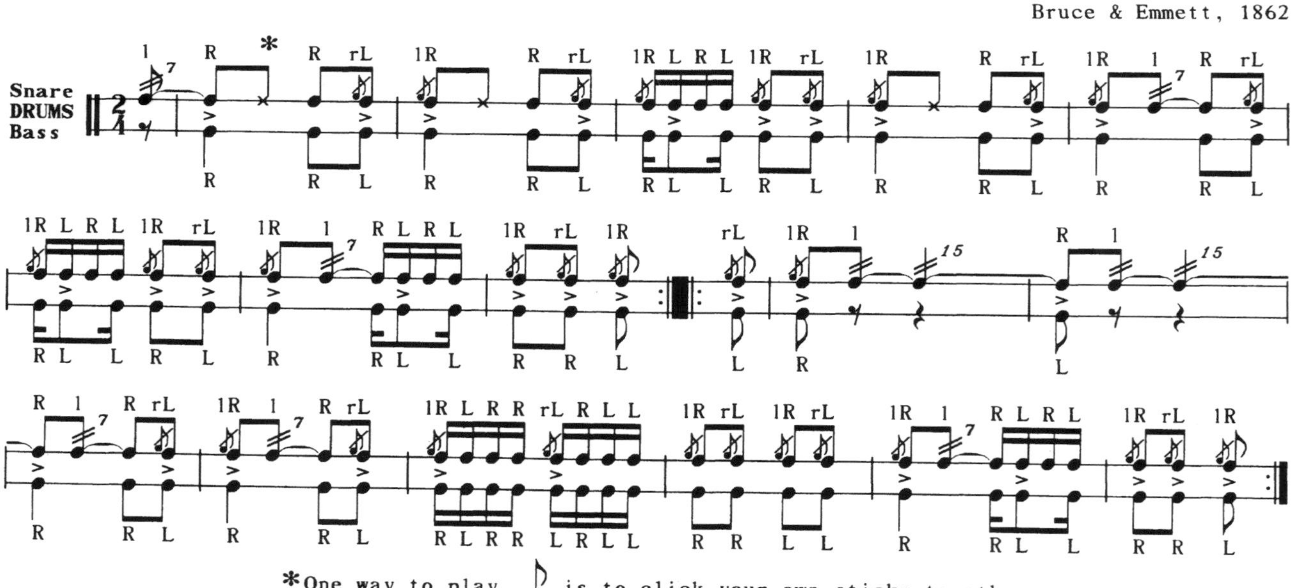

Garry Owen

Concert-Pitch Chords:
Traditional
FIFE I
Repeat
End
Fife-Pitch Chords:
Walter D. Sweet
FIFE II
Repeat
End
Traditional
Snare DRUMS Bass
Plain Six-Eight

Columbia, the Gem of the Ocean

The Yellow Rose of Texas
Concert-Pitch Chords:
Traditional
FIFE I
Fife-Pitch Chords:
FIFE II
Suggested drumbeat for both tunes: Connecticut Halftime, pp.10 & 11.
The Blue and the Gray
Paul Dresser [1900]; traditionalized
Concert-Pitch Chords:
FIFE I
Fife-Pitch Chords:
FIFE II

Connecticut Halftime

(A) Hart's transcription shows no flam at these places.

(B) Hart's transcription shows a *Single-Seven* here.

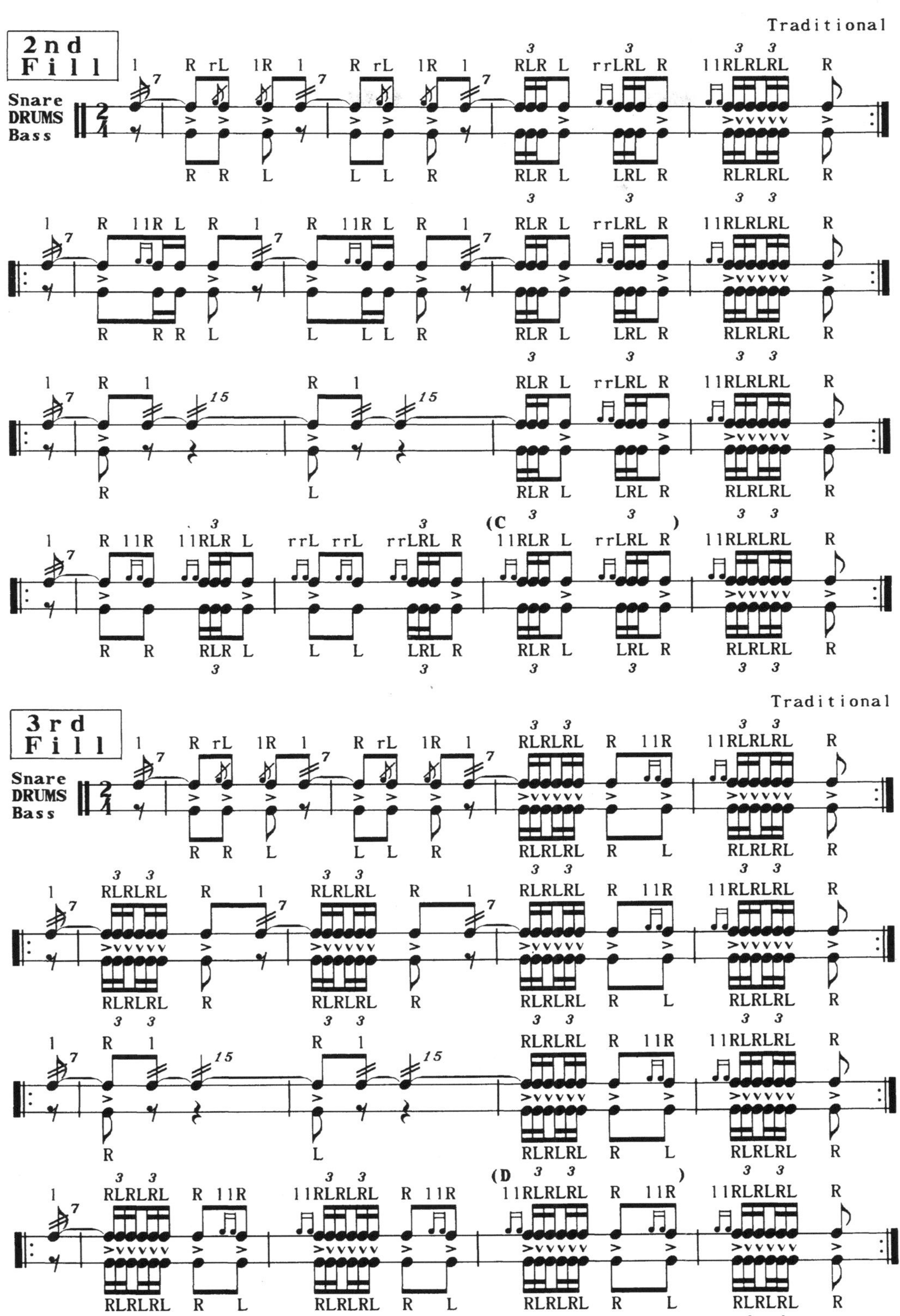

Instead of **(D)**, some drummers repeat **(C)** as above.

Rally 'Round the Flag

Suggested drumbeat: *Connecticut Halftime*, pp 10 & 11

Old Dan Tucker

For Fife II and the drumbeat, see facing page

Old Dan Tucker Continued

Stonewall Jackson's Way

Suggested drumbeat: *Army Six-Eight*, below.

Army Six-Eight

A general-purpose drumbeat

WESTBROOK (CT) ANCIENT MUSTER 4TH SATURDAY IN AUGUST

Goober Peas

Concert-Pitch Chords:
Traditional
FIFE I
G D7 G C G D7 G C D7 G D7 G C G C G D7 G G C D7 G C G D7 G
Fife-Pitch Chords:
Walter D. Sweet
FIFE II
E♭ B♭7 E♭ A♭ E♭ B♭7 A♭ B♭7 E♭ B♭7 E♭ A♭ E♭ A♭ E♭ B♭7 E♭ E♭ A♭ B♭7 E♭ A♭ E♭ B♭7 E♭

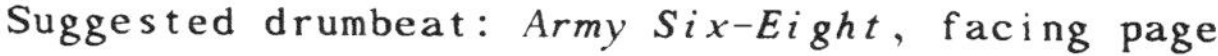
Suggested drumbeat: *Army Six-Eight*, facing page

The Bonnie Blue Flag
Concert-Pitch Chords:
Traditional
FIFE I
G C G D7 G C G D7 G G D C G D7 G
Fife-Pitch Chords:
Walter D. Sweet
FIFE II
E♭ A♭ E♭ B♭7 E♭ A♭ E♭ B♭7 E♭ E♭ B♭ A♭ E♭ B♭7 E♭
Suggested drumbeat: *Army Six-Eight*, facing page.

Dixie
Concert-Pitch Chords:
Daniel D. Emmett, 1858
FIFE I
Fife-Pitch Chords:
Walter D. Sweet
FIFE II
George B. Bruce, 1862
Snare
DRUMS
Bass

Just Before the Battle, Mother

Concert-Pitch Chords:

George F. Root, 1864: traditionalized

FIFE I

D G A7 D

D G A7 D *Fine*

D G E7 A7 *D.S. al Fine*

Fife-Pitch Chords:

Walter D. Sweet

II FIFE III

Bb Eb F7 Bb

Eb F7 Bb Bb Eb C7

F7 Bb Eb F7 Bb

pp FIFE III *f* FIFE II FIFE II FIFE III

Popular drumbeat, *Connecticut Halftime*, pp.10 & 11, ♩=106. Alternate drumbeat below, ♩=90.

Brian Seibel & Walter D. Sweet

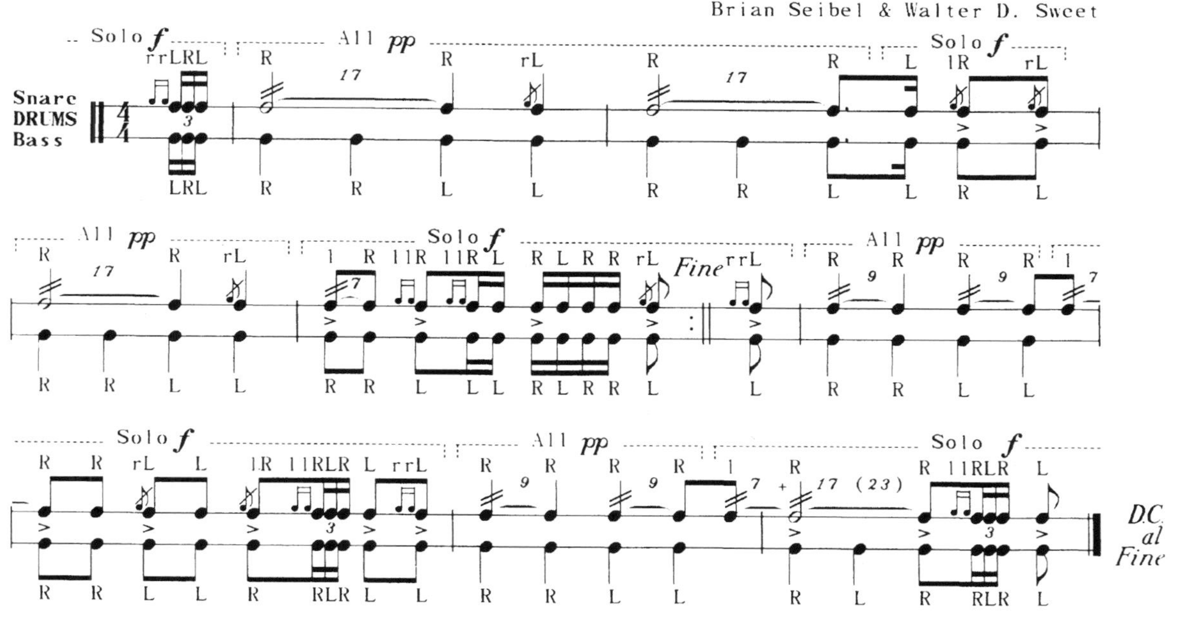

End of tune (marked Solo) all play *pp* < *ff*
This drumbeat also appropriate for *Onward Christian Soldiers* (play AABBAB)

Finnegan's Wake
Traditional
Concert-Pitch Chords:
FIFE I
Walter D. Sweet
Fife-Pitch Chords:
FIFE II
Suggested drumbeat: Monumental Two-Four, below.
Monumental Two-Four
A general-purpose drumbeat
Bruce & Emmett, 1862
Snare DRUMS Bass

The Wearin' of the Green

The Minstrel Boy

*For alternate sticking in these places, see *Fancy Six-Eight*, p.35.

Note: See p.78, *Tearful Drummer*. The footnote gives instructions for performing the Slow March.

Marching Through Georgia

The Kingdom Coming

Henry C. Work, 1862

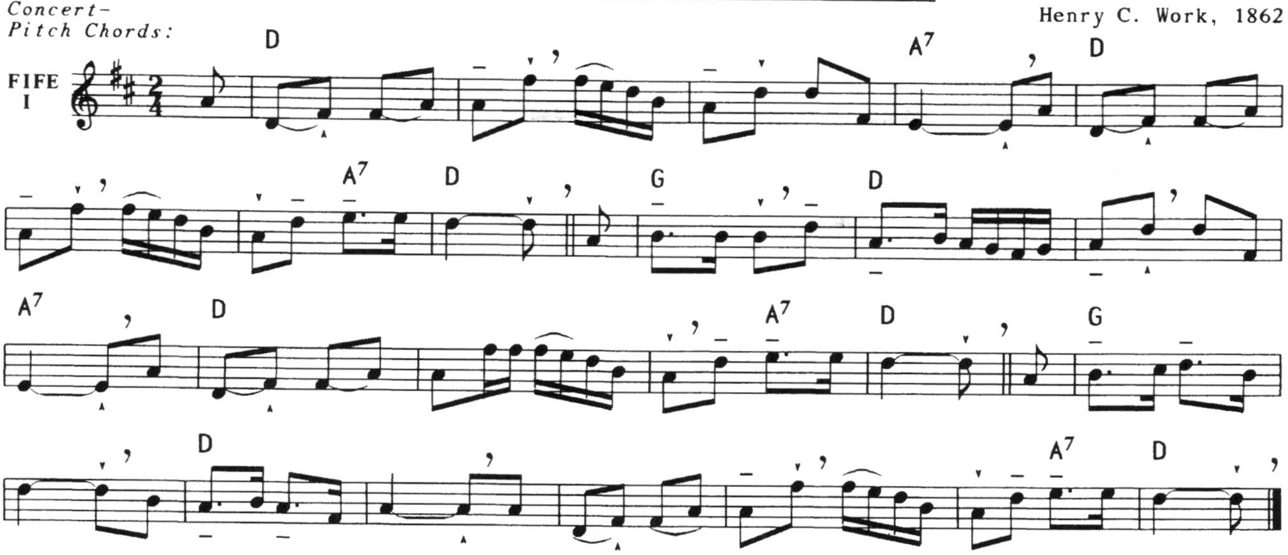
Concert-
Pitch Chords:
FIFE
I
D
A7
G

Walter D. Sweet

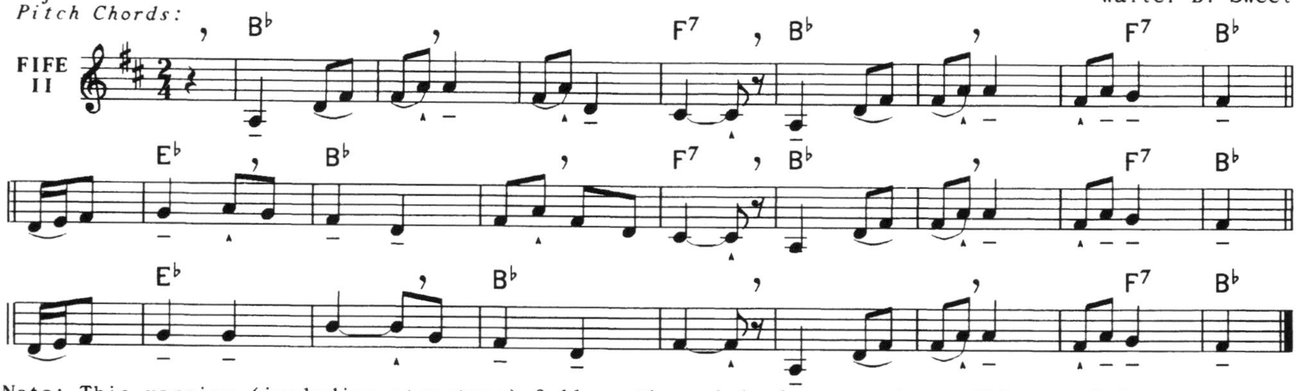
Fife-
Pitch Chords:
FIFE
II
B♭
F7
E♭

Note: This version (including structure) follows the original song. Among fifers and drummers, versions vary. Some corps repeat the 3rd strain; the author suggests repeating the 1st strain, due to the similarity of the 2nd and 3rd. Suggested drumbeat, *Ancient & Honorable Artillery* (below)

Ancient & Honorable Artillery

Bruce & Emmett, 1862

Snare
DRUMS
Bass

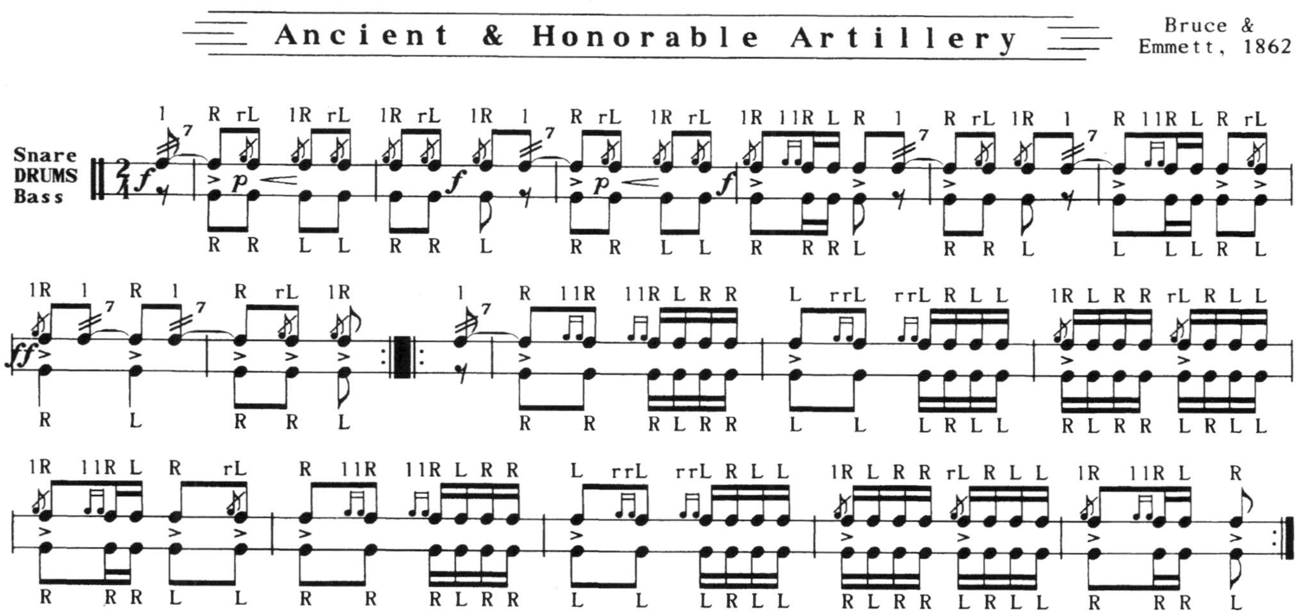

Grandfather's Clock

Henry C. Work, 1877; traditionalized

Walter D. Sweet

For the drumbeat, see facing page. Regarding X and Y, see the Slow March on p.78

East Hampton Fifes & Drums

Streetbeat

Composed by James M. Clark. Used by permission of East Hampton Fifes and Drums

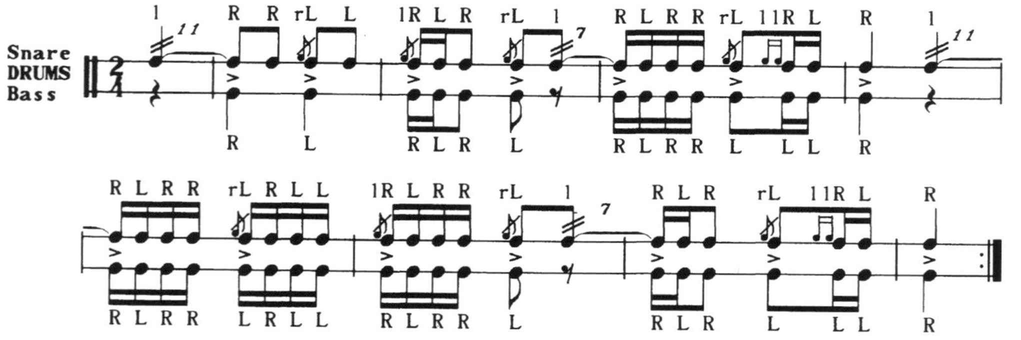

Grandfather's Clock Continued

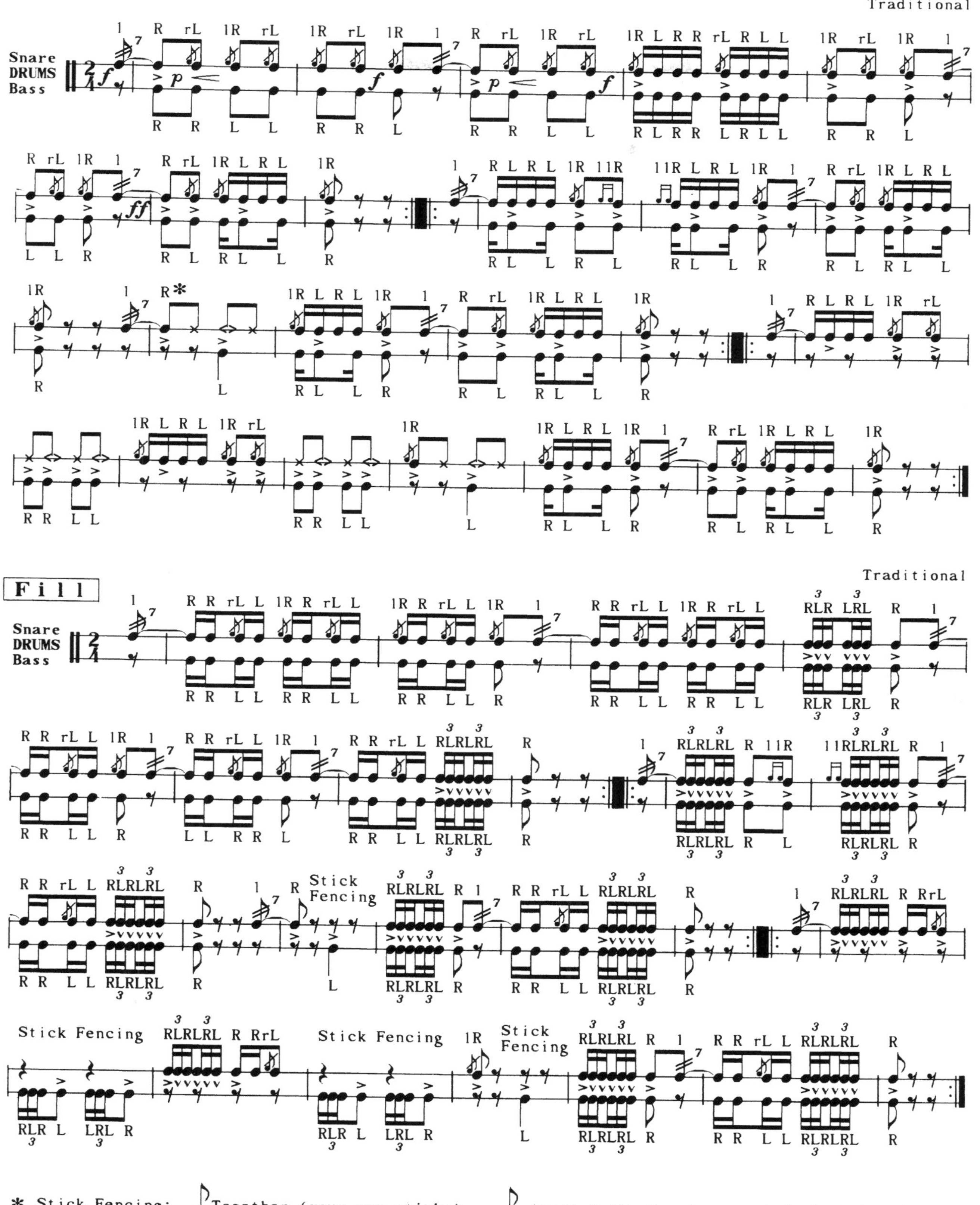

* Stick Fencing: Together (your own sticks) Apart (with the drummer left & right of you)

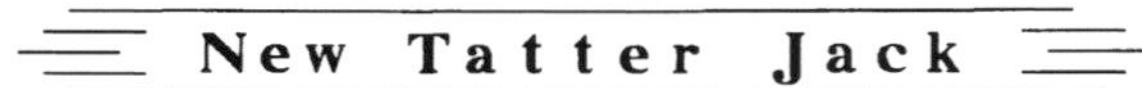

New Tatter Jack

Traditional

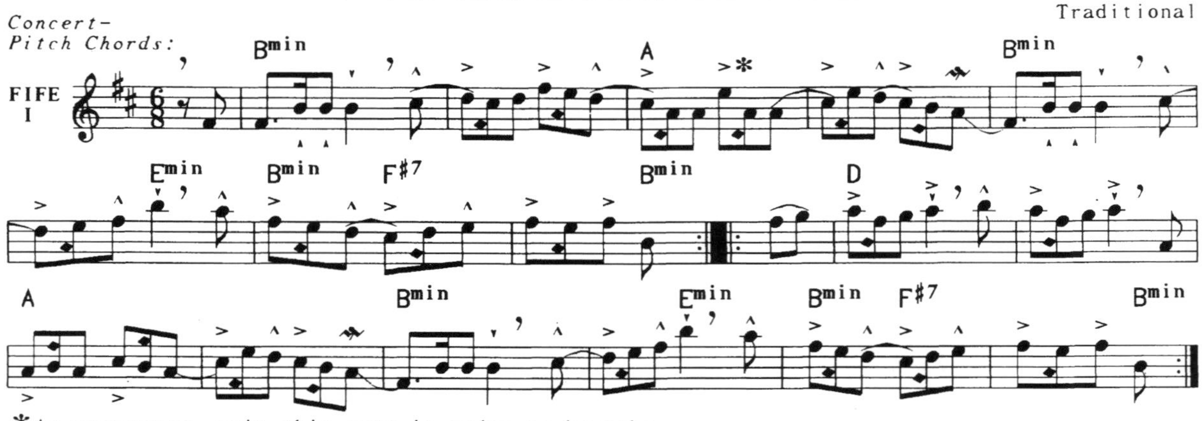
Concert-
Pitch Chords:
FIFE I
Bmin
A
Bmin
Emin
Bmin
F#7
Bmin
D
A
Bmin
Emin
Bmin
F#7
Bmin

*As necessary, omit this note in order to breathe

Walter D. Sweet

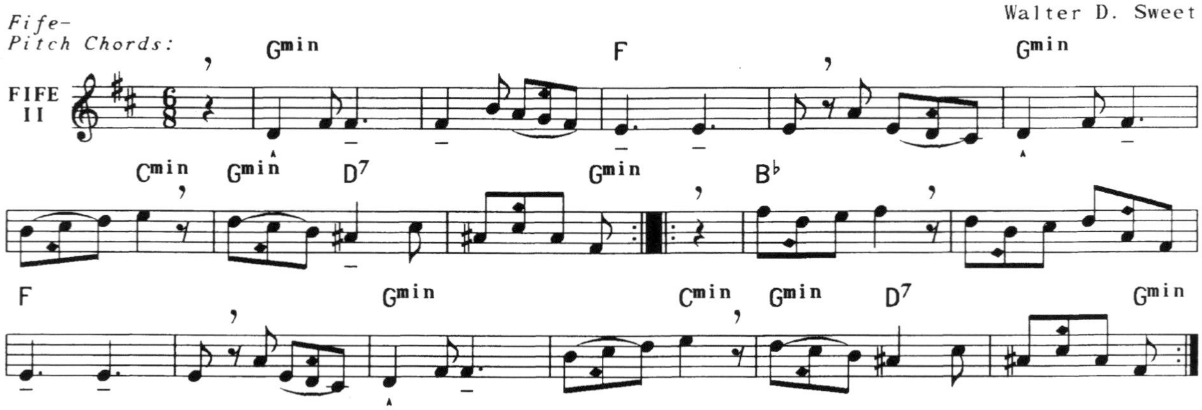
Fife-
Pitch Chords:
FIFE II
Gmin
F
Gmin
Cmin
Gmin
D7
Gmin
B♭
F
Gmin
Cmin
Gmin
D7
Gmin

Suggested drumbeat for both tunes: *Plain Six-Eight*, facing page.

Tallewan

Traditional

Concert-
Pitch Chords:
FIFE I
G
D7
G
C
D7
G
G
C
G
D7
G
C
G
D7
G

Walter D. Sweet

Fife-
Pitch Chords:
FIFE II
E♭
B♭7
E♭
A♭
B♭7
E♭
E♭
A♭
E♭
B♭7
E♭
A♭
E♭
B♭7
E♭

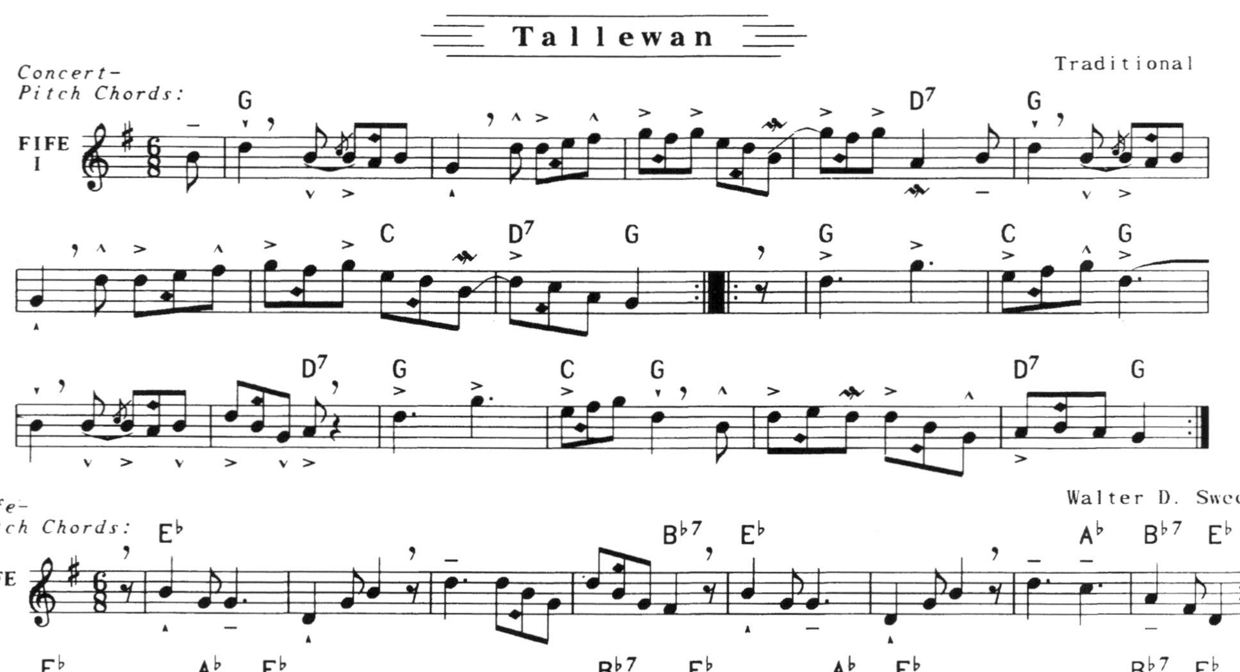

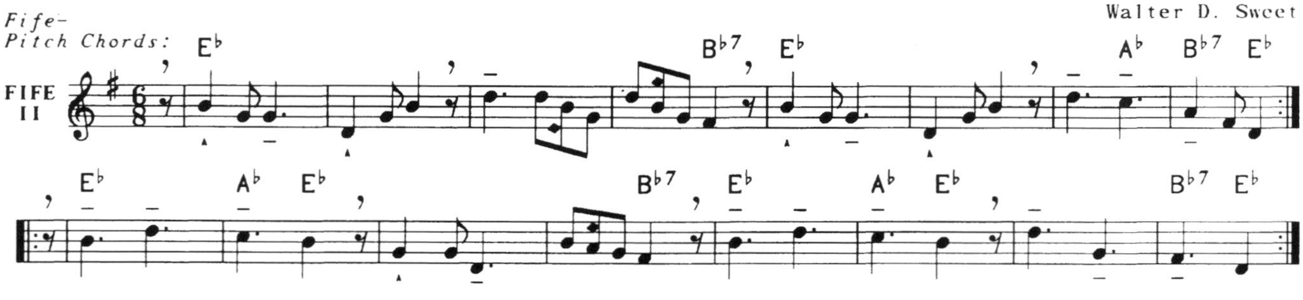

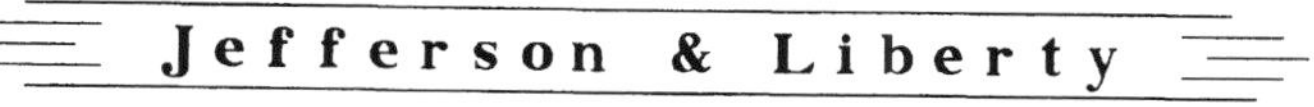

Jefferson & Liberty

Concert-Pitch Chords:

Traditional

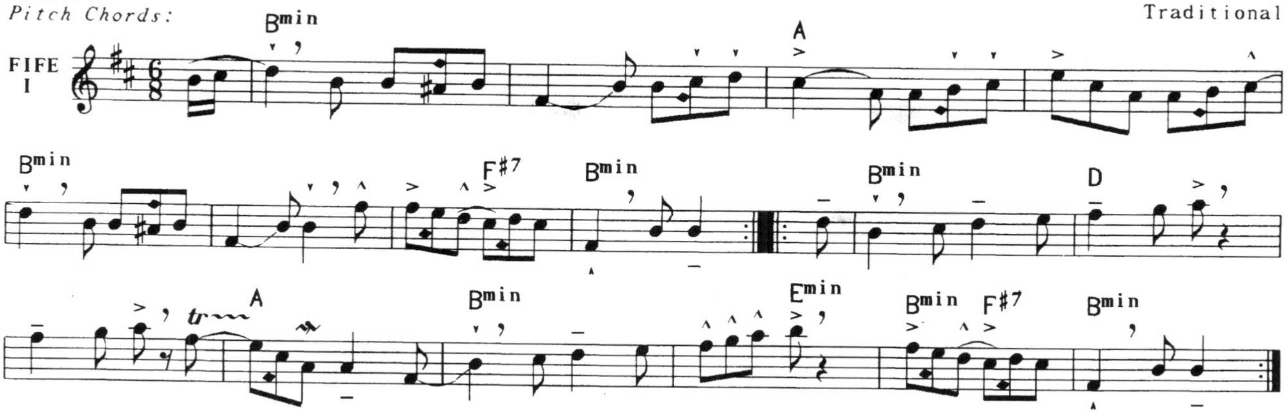
FIFE I
Bmin
A
Bmin
F#7
Bmin
Bmin
D
A
Bmin
Emin
Bmin
F#7
Bmin

Fife-Pitch Chords:

Walter D. Sweet

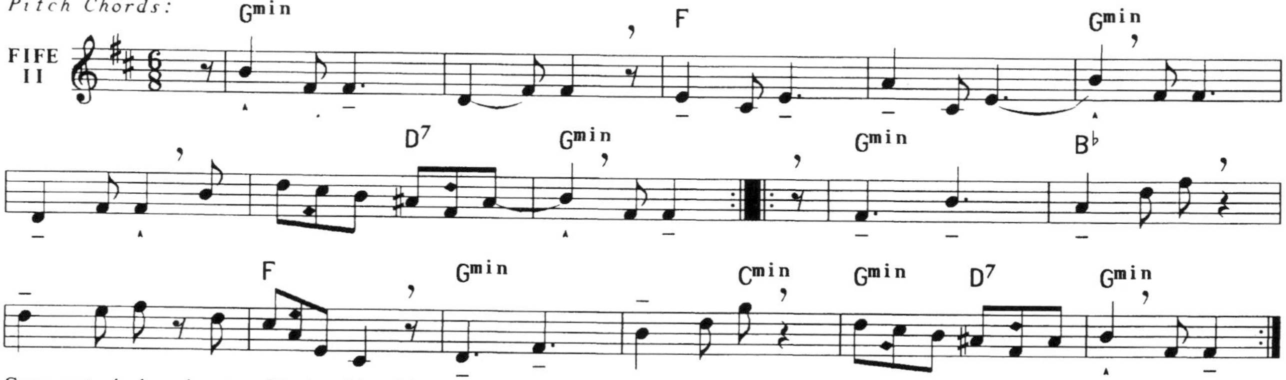
FIFE II
Gmin
F
Gmin
D7
Gmin
Gmin
B♭
F
Gmin
Cmin
Gmin
D7
Gmin

Suggested drumbeat: *Plain Six-Eight,* below.

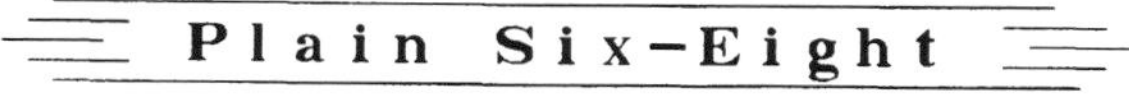

Plain Six-Eight

A general-purpose drumbeat

Traditional

Snare
DRUMS
Bass

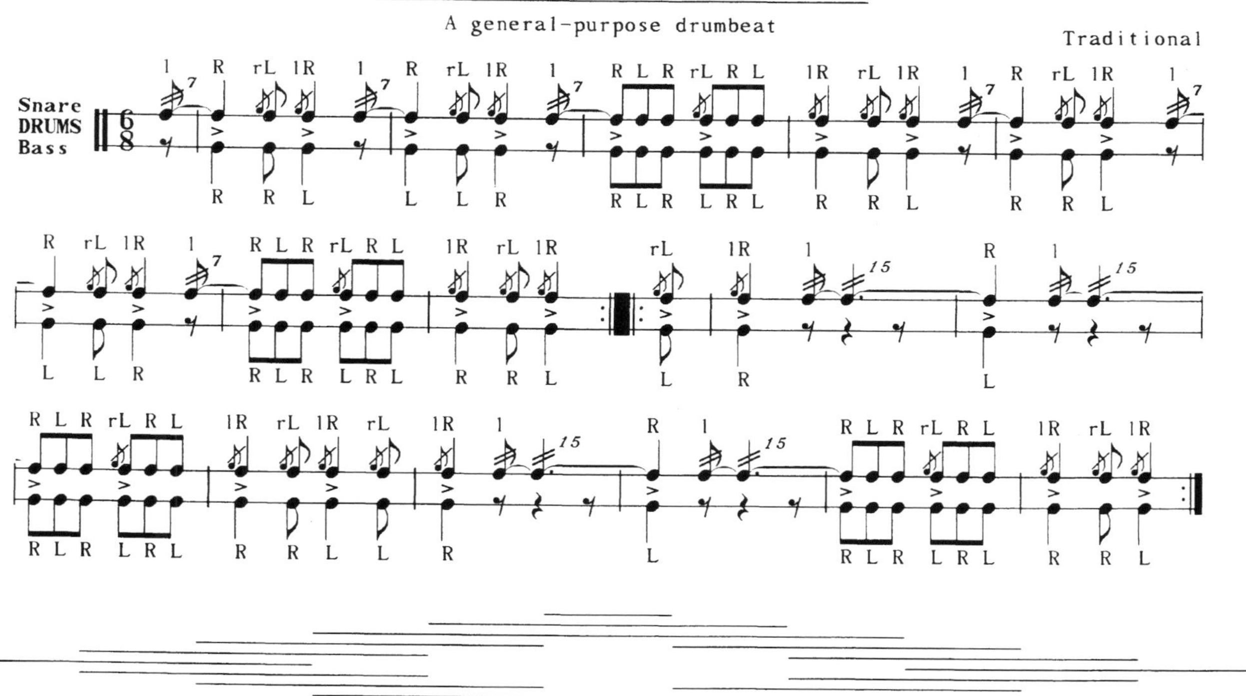

The British Grenadiers

Suggested drumbeats, *Road to Boston*, facing page, or *Army Two-Four*, p.5.

The Road to Boston

For the drumbeat, see facing page. Alternate drumbeat, *Army Two-Four*, p.5

The Road to Boston

Ostling, 1939

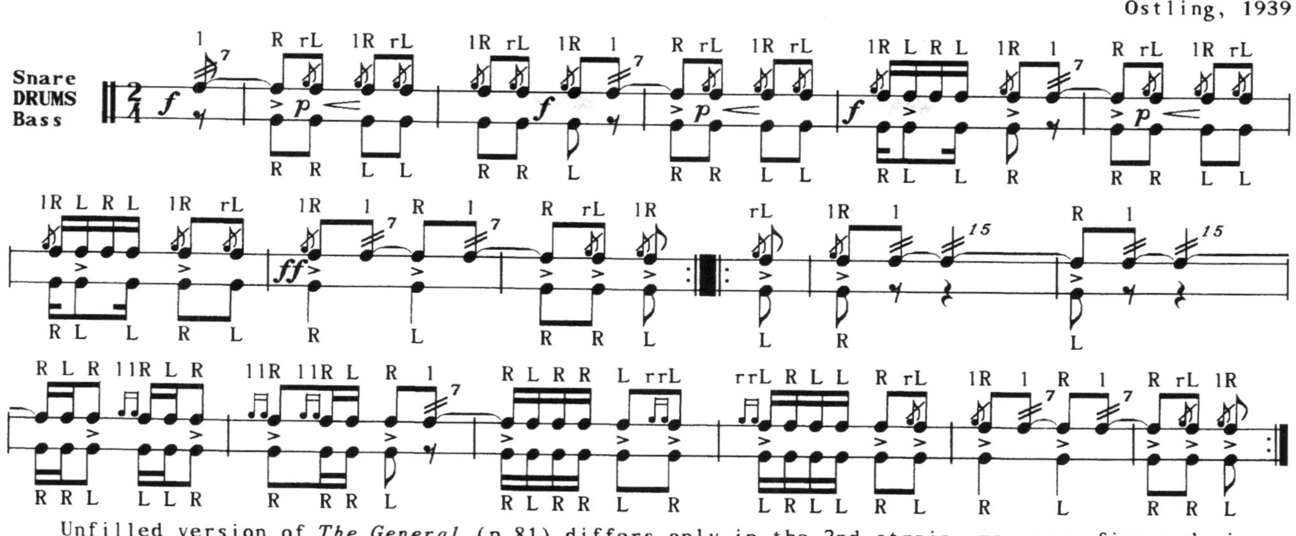

Unfilled version of *The General* (p.81) differs only in the 2nd strain, measures five and six

Ostling, 1939

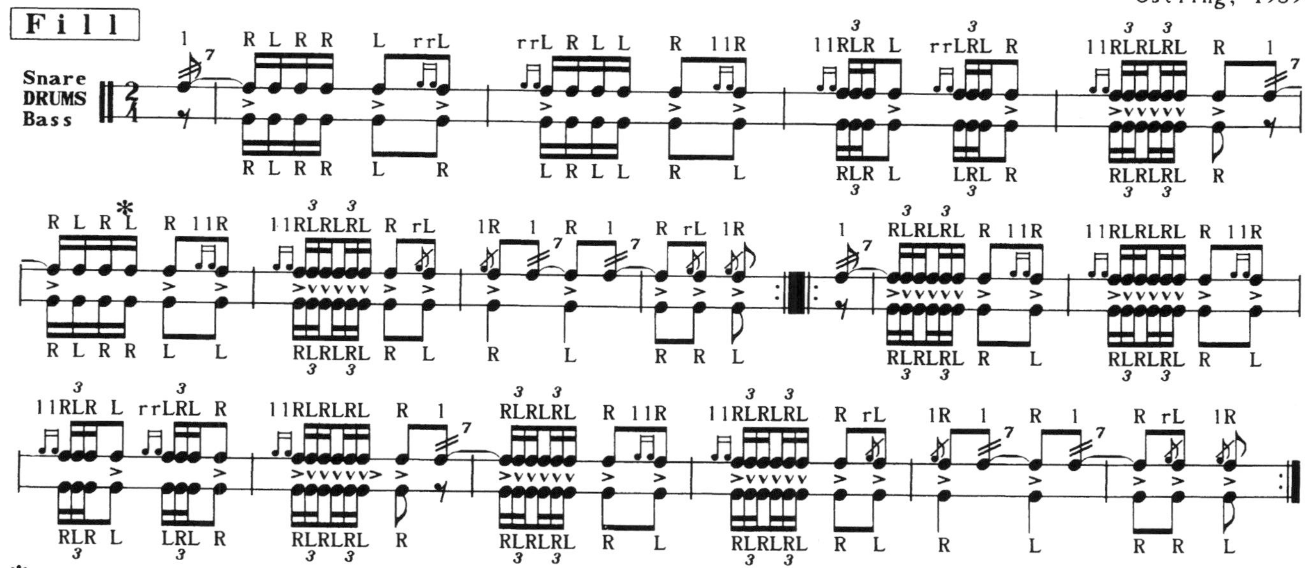

*Note the sticking and accent (not a rudiment).

Westbrook Drum Corps

Streetbeat

Used by permission

*No flam

The Downfall of Paris

Concert-Pitch Chords:

Bruce & Emmett, 1862

FIFE I

For **FIFE II** and the drumbeat, see pp.31 and 32.

*Eighth notes alone: play at full face value

Fife Fingering Chart

Continued next page

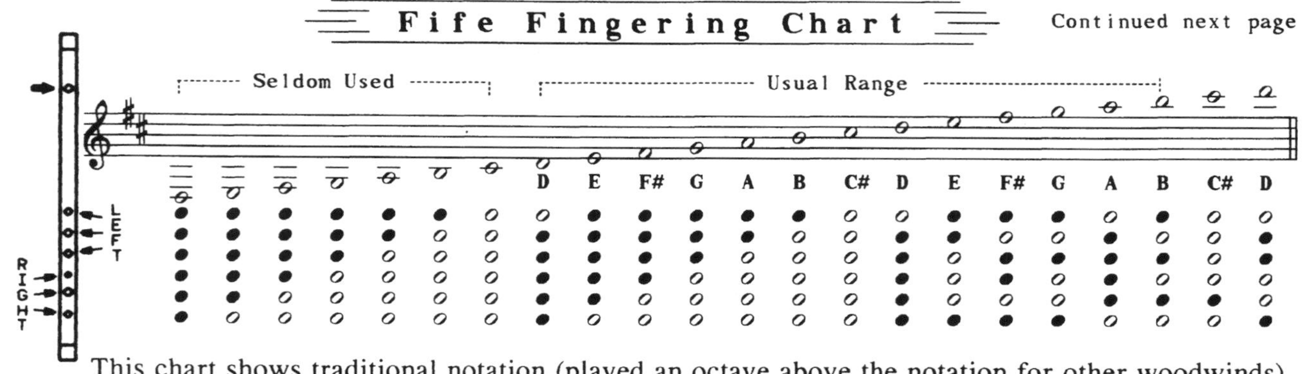

This chart shows traditional notation (played an octave above the notation for other woodwinds)

The Downfall of Paris

Continued

* Not effective on all fifes.

@ Open or closed to suit the fife.

% Better in tune, not standard; sometimes unclear or unstable.

Note: For Ornaments, use trill fingerings.

Bruce & Emmett, 1862

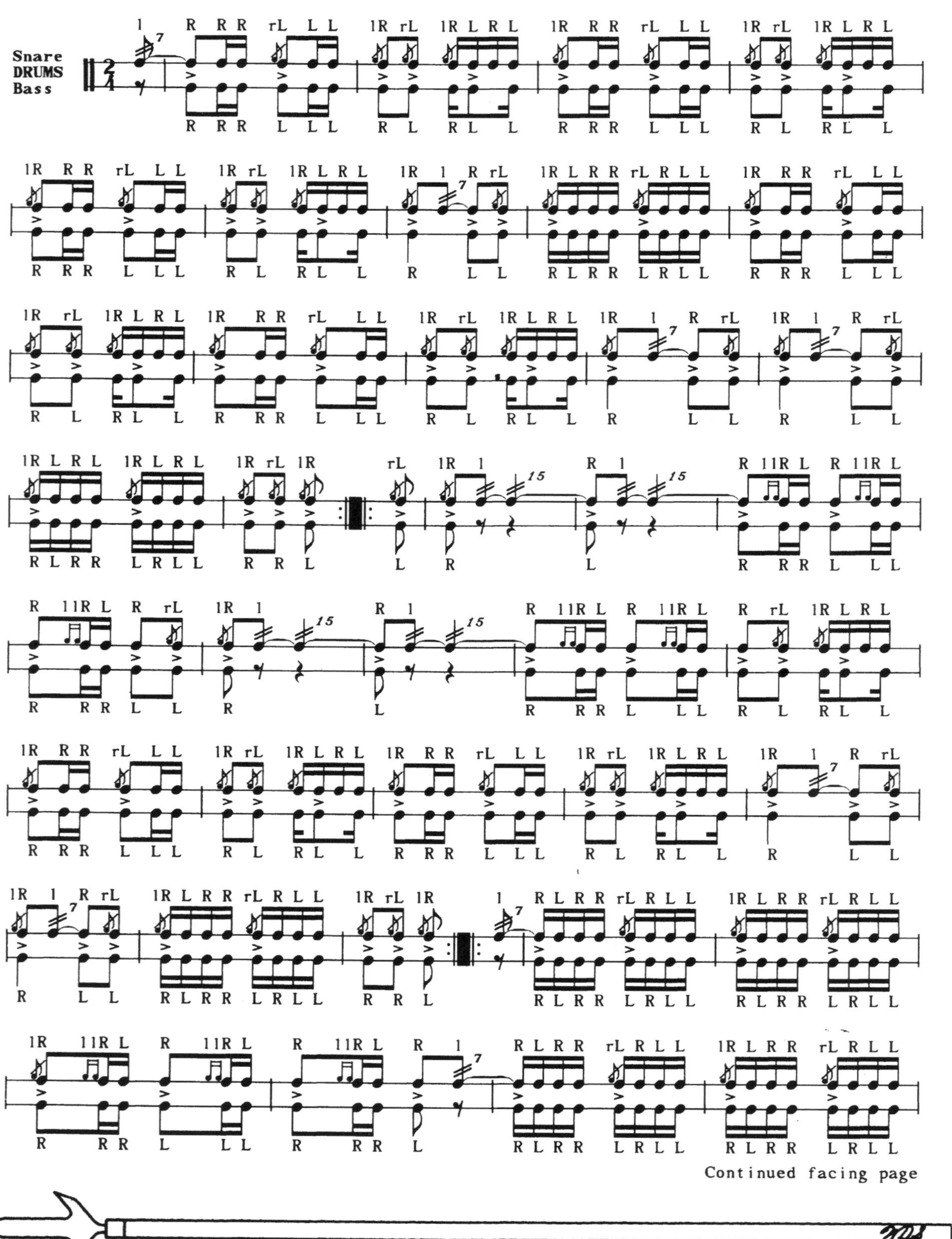

Continued facing page

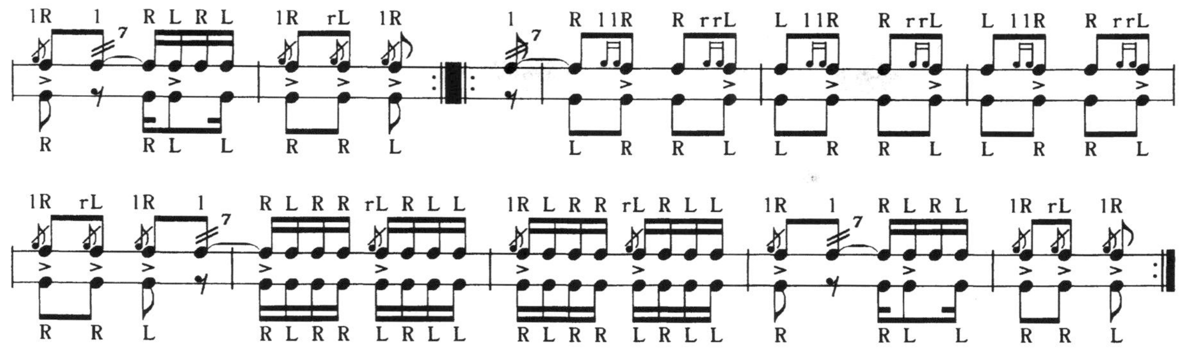

The Eighth Volunteers

Streetbeat (1979)

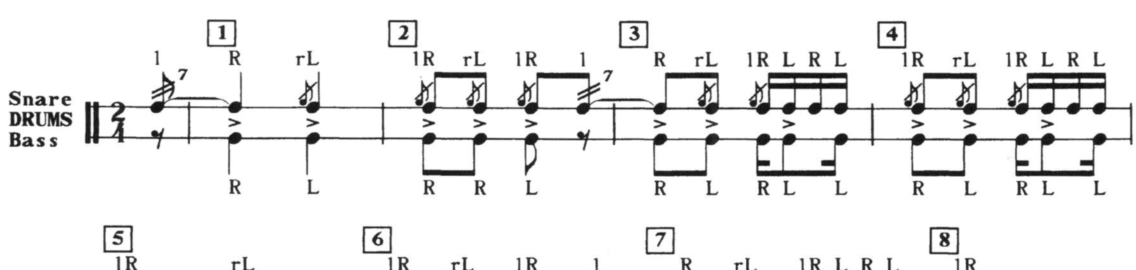

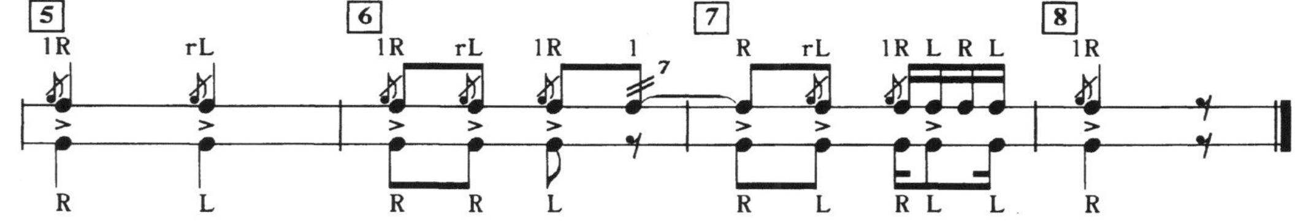

Starting a Tune from the Streetbeat

See the streetbeat above. When the start of the tune has been announced, play measures 5 thru 8 as follows (this plan involves no separate rolloff):

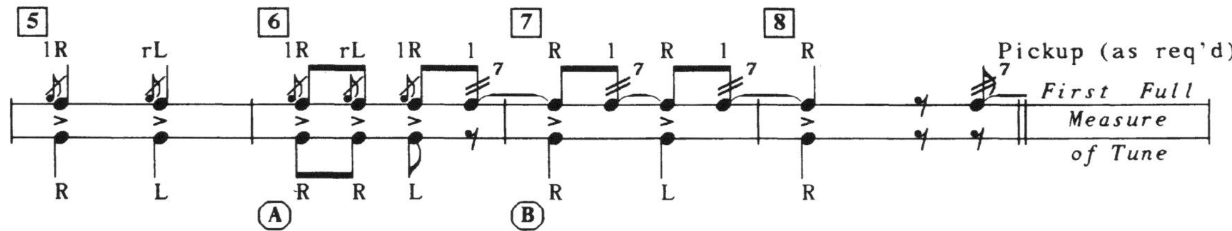

Fifers assume the playing position as follows: The right hand raises the fife to the face; the fife reaches final position at point A.. The left hand reaches the fife at point B.

Precision of drill varies from corps to corps. Some corps play a rolloff or other introduction to the tune; other corps lead in directly from the streetbeat without any changes.

City Guards
Traditional
Concert-Pitch Chords:
FIFE I
Fife-Pitch Chords:
Walter D. Sweet
FIFE II
Suggested drumbeat for both tunes, *Fancy Six-Eight*, facing page
Father O'Flynn
Traditional
Concert-Pitch Chords:
FIFE I
*As necessary, omit these notes in order to breathe
Walter D. Sweet
Fife-Pitch Chords:
FIFE II

Fifty Cents
Concert-Pitch Chords:
Traditional
FIFE I
Repeat
End
Fife-Pitch Chords:
Walter D. Sweet
FIFE II
Suggested drumbeat, Fancy Six-Eight, below
Fancy Six-Eight
A general-purpose drumbeat
Traditional
Snare DRUMS Bass
Alternate Sticking
1st strain:
2nd strain:
Measure #4
Back to 2nd strain
To 1st strain or end

Old Saybrook

Concert-Pitch Chords:

Traditional

FIFE I

Fife-Pitch Chords:

Walter D. Sweet

FIFE II

For the drumbeat, see facing page.

NOTE: These transcriptions call for two iterations of the 3rd strain. Some musicians play it a third and fourth time.

Below: Filled version, 3rd strain, 2nd ending

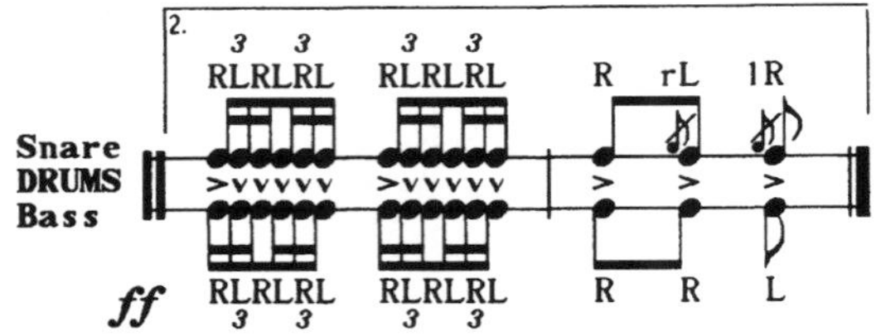

Old Saybrook — Continued

For the 3rd strain, play the unfilled version except for the second ending shown on the facing page

Irish Reel

Concert-Pitch Chords:
Traditional
FIFE I
D
A7
The Rakes of Mallow
Fife-Pitch Chords:
Walter D. Sweet
FIFE II
B♭
F7
Traditional
Snare DRUMS Bass

Eighteen–Twelve

* In the strict Rudimental style, this *Flam* completes the *Flamacue*. The original *Hashup* deviates in these places by calling for a *Tap* (single stroke) in place of the *Flam*. In the author's opinion, the *Flam* is musically effective without compromising the *Flamacue*.

Martin's Rattler

Oyster River Hornpipe

Paddy O'Toole

Traditional

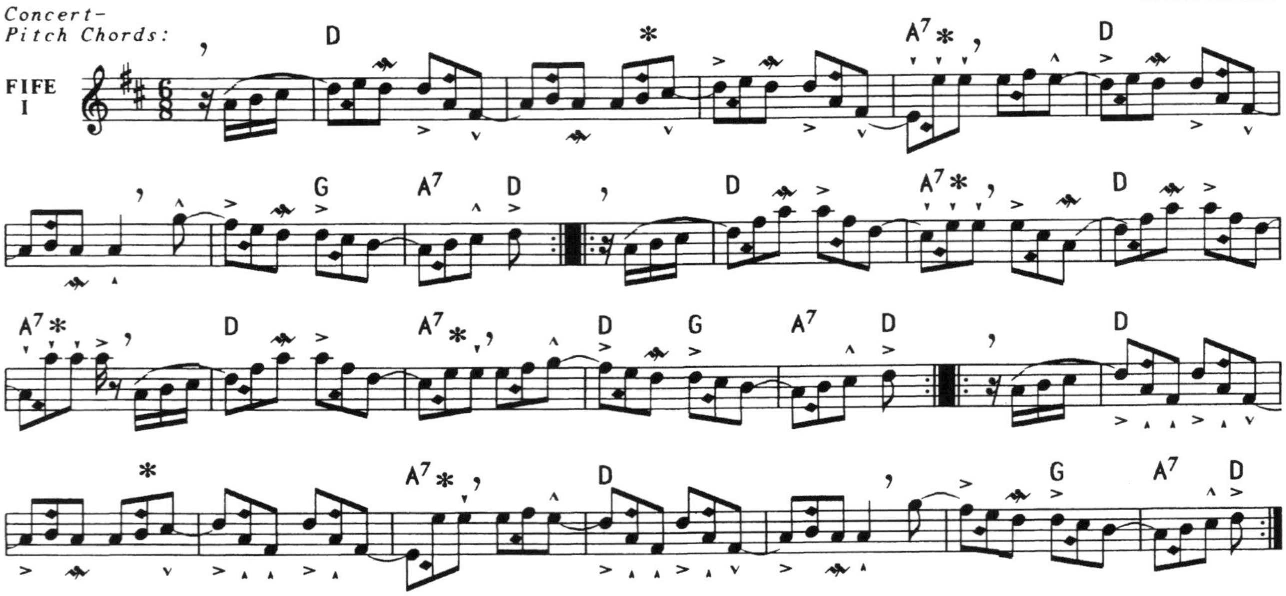

Concert-Pitch Chords:

FIFE I

D A7 D G A7 D D A7 D A7 D A7 D G A7 D D A7 D G A7 D

*As necessary, omit these notes in order to breathe

Walter D. Sweet

Fife-Pitch Chords:

FIFE II

B♭ F7 B♭ E♭ F7 B♭ B♭ F7 B♭ F7 B♭ F7 B♭ E♭ F7 B♭ B♭ F7 B♭ E♭ F7 B♭

For the drumbeat, see facing page

Flam Rolloff

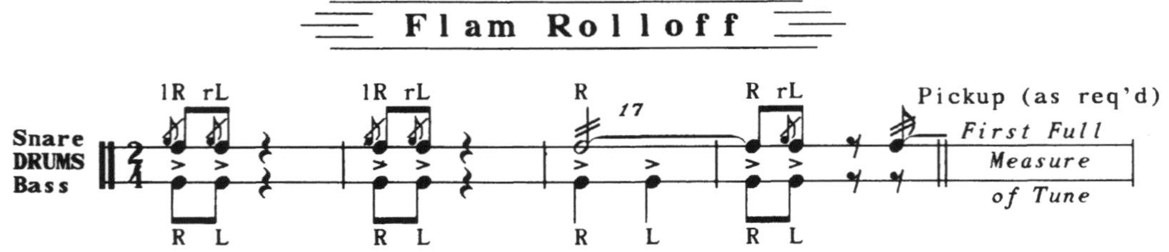

The Rolloff signals the start of the tune, starting either from silence, or from another piece of music such as the streetbeat. Sometimes, the lead drummer starts the rolloff, then the other drummers join in. *Rolloff* meter is always 2/4, even when the tune is in 6/8.

Paddy O'Toole Continued

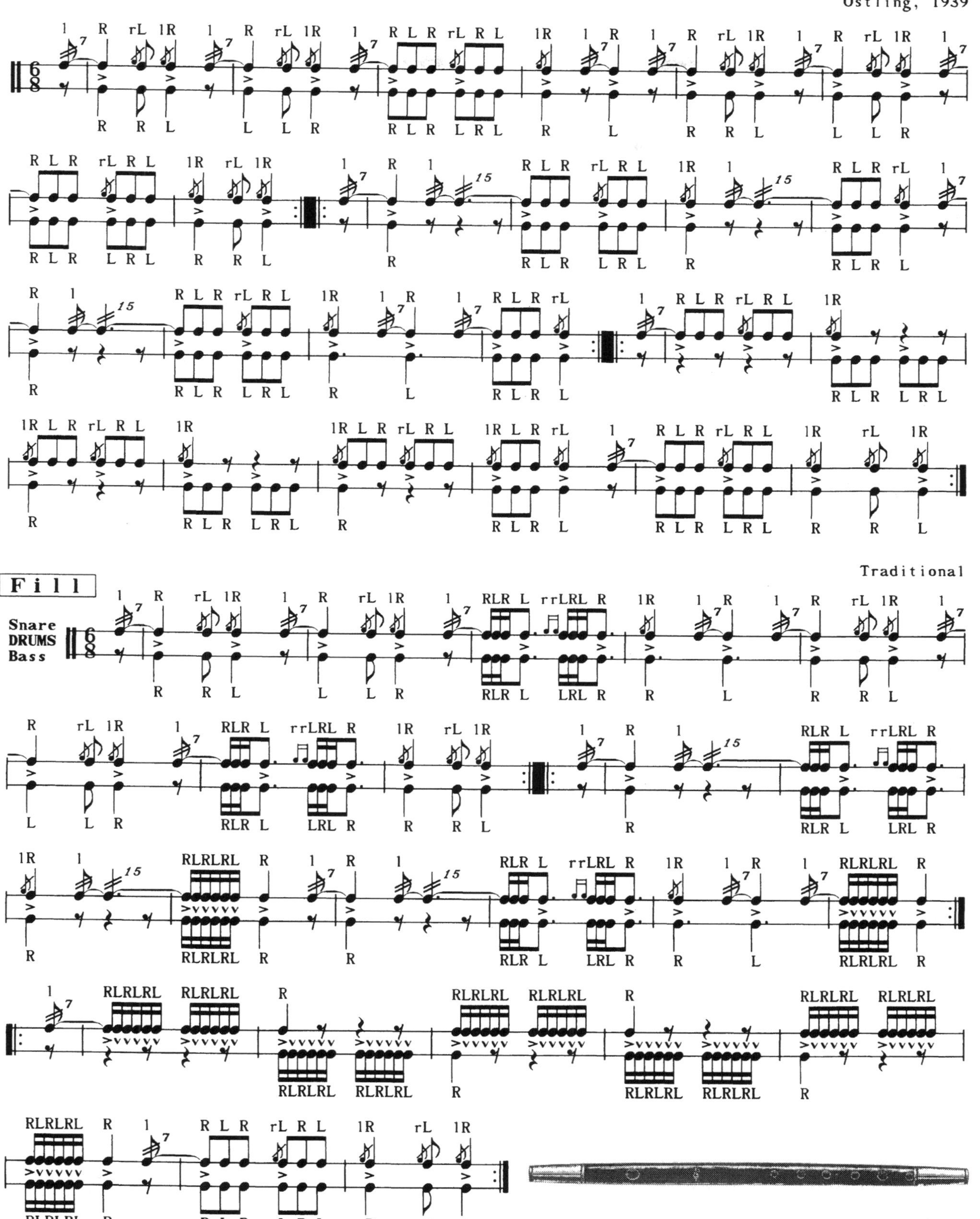

The Jaybird

Traditional
Concert-
Pitch Chords:
FIFE I
Walter D. Sweet
Fife-
Pitch Chords:
FIFE II
Traditional
Snare
DRUMS
Bass

Fireman's Quickstep

York Fusiliers

For the drumbeat, see facing page

York Fusiliers Continued

Carroll Collection Vol II, c. 1965
Used by permission

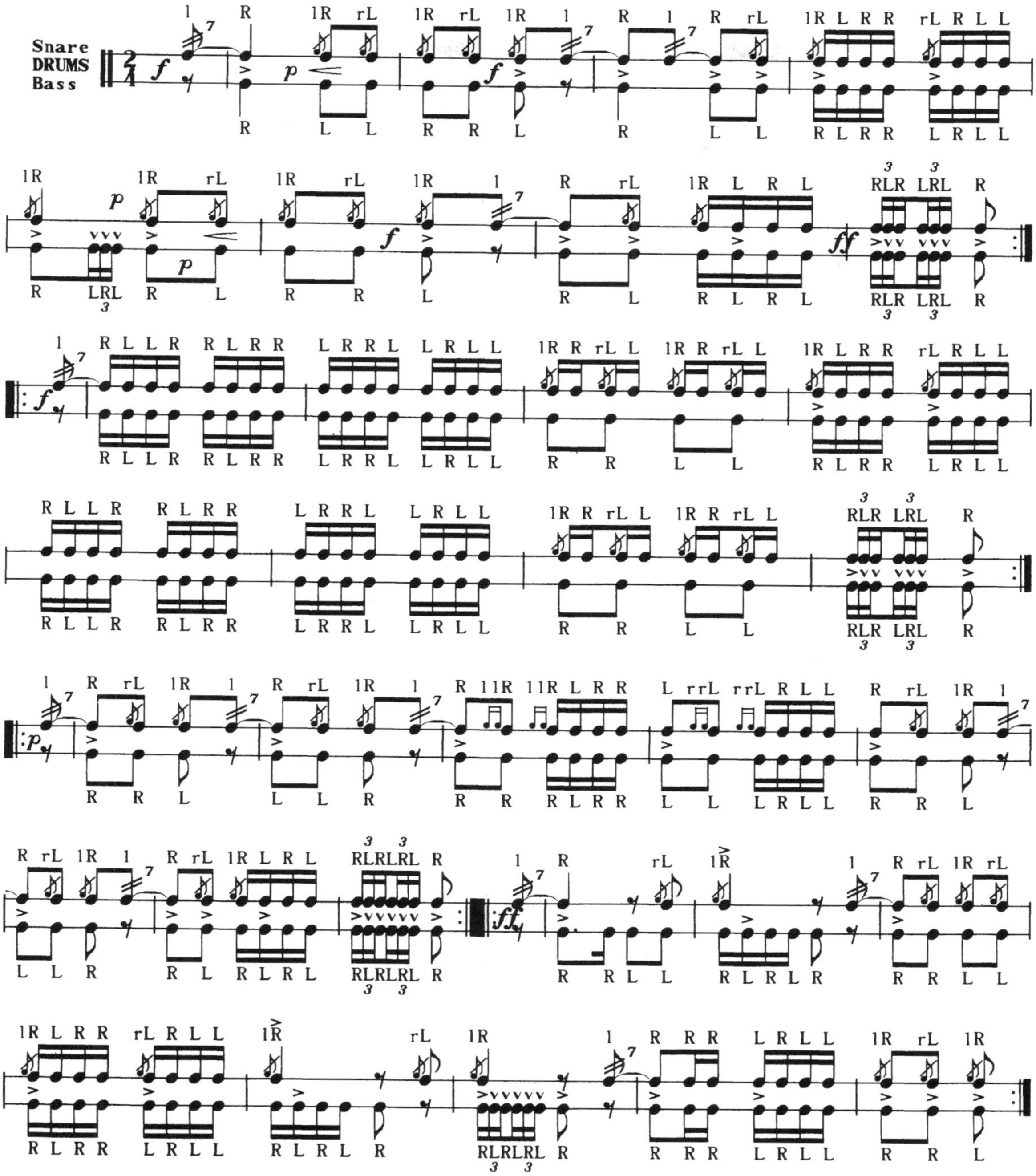
Snare
DRUMS
Bass

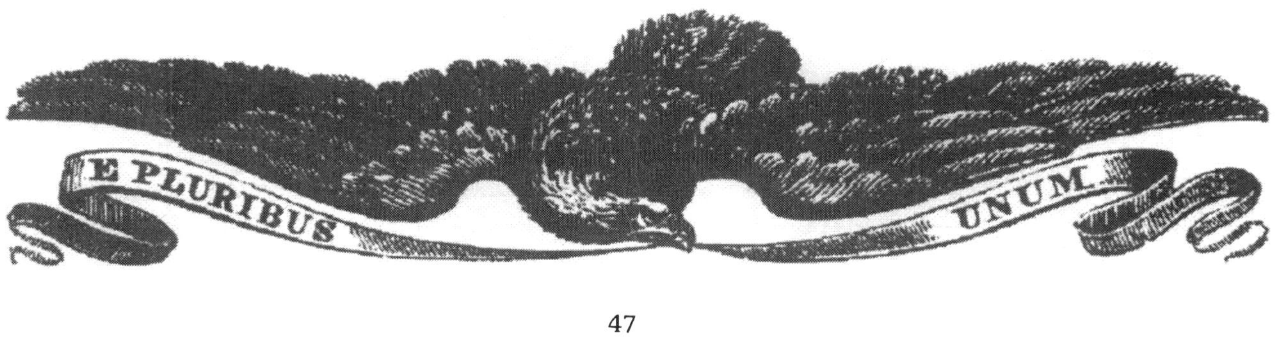
E PLURIBUS UNUM

Sisters

Concert-Pitch Chords:
Ostling, 1939
FIFE I
Fife-Pitch Chords:
Walter D. Sweet
FIFE II
A general-purpose drumbeat
Sisters
Ostling, 1939
Snare DRUMS Bass
Fill
Traditional
Snare DRUMS Bass
At the third measure of both strains, take out the Flam Accents
and play Single Ratamacues

Blackberry Quadrille

Huntington

Concert-Pitch Chords:
Colin Sterne, 1938
Used by permission
FIFE I
Fife-Pitch Chords:
Walter D. Sweet
FIFE II
Harmony for the 3rd strain, see above
Francis Goss, 1938
Used by permission
Snare DRUMS Bass

Some Distance from Prussia

Essence of Tampa

Traditional

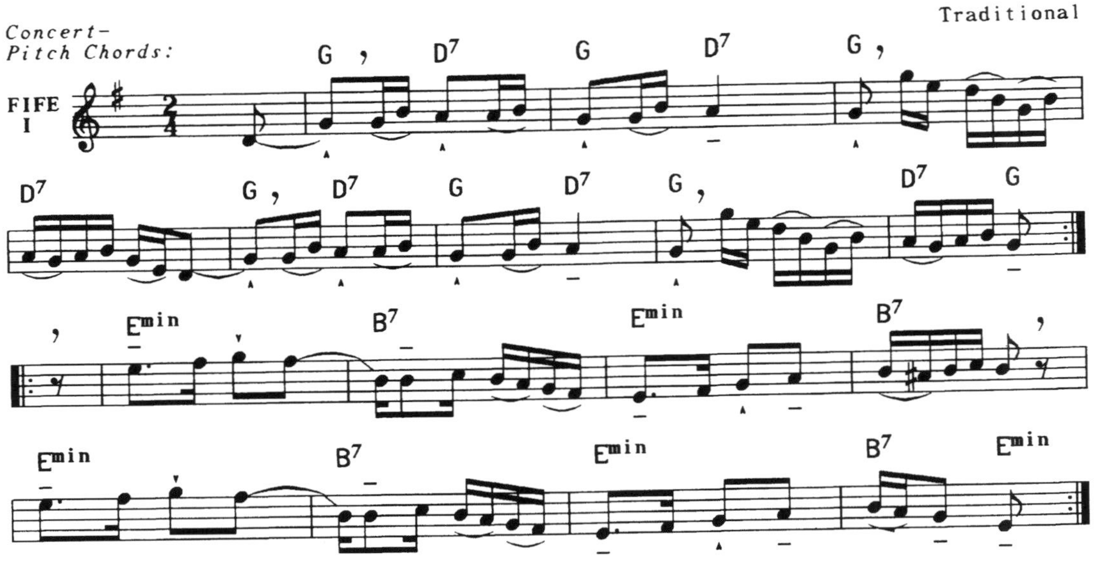
Concert-
Pitch Chords:
FIFE I
G D7 G D7 G
D7 G D7 G D7 G D7 G
Emin B7 Emin B7
Emin B7 Emin B7 Emin

Walter D. Sweet

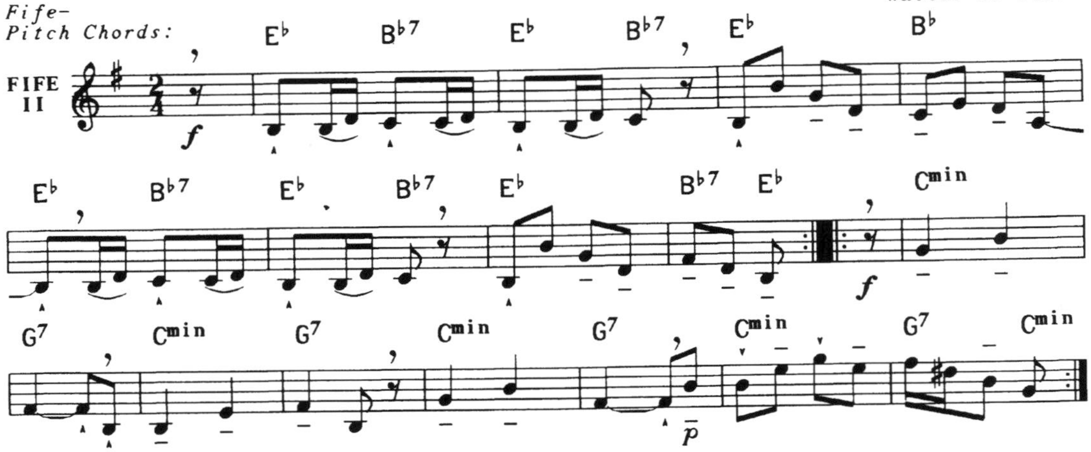
Fife-
Pitch Chords:
FIFE II
Eb Bb7 Eb Bb7 Eb Bb
Eb Bb7 Eb Bb7 Eb Bb7 Eb Cmin
G7 Cmin G7 Cmin G7 Cmin G7 Cmin

Suggested drumbeat, *Paddy On a Handcar*, facing page

Paddy on a Handcar

Traditional

Concert-
Pitch Chords:
FIFE I
Amin Emin Amin
G Amin Amin G
Amin G Amin G Amin

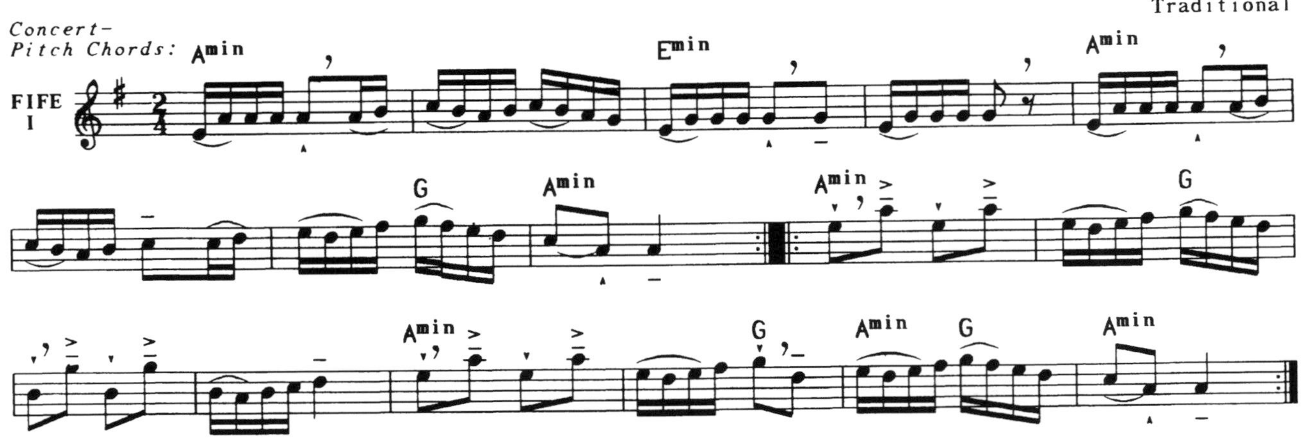

For **FIFE II** and the drumbeat, see facing page

Paddy on a Handcar — Continued

The Village Quickstep

FIFE II, C-strain is traditional. For the drumbeat, see facing page.

The Village Quickstep

Continued

Ostling, 1939

Snare
DRUMS
Bass

* It is the author's intent to document actual field practices at the time of this writing. In this figure, the rhythm varies greatly. Some players use the rhythm transcribed above. Others lengthen the first note to a dotted eighth, while the snare drummers take time for a flam. Effectively, this switches the meter to 2/4 for one beat, then back to 6/8 while the tempo goes unchanged. This switch is shown in the next four transcriptions:

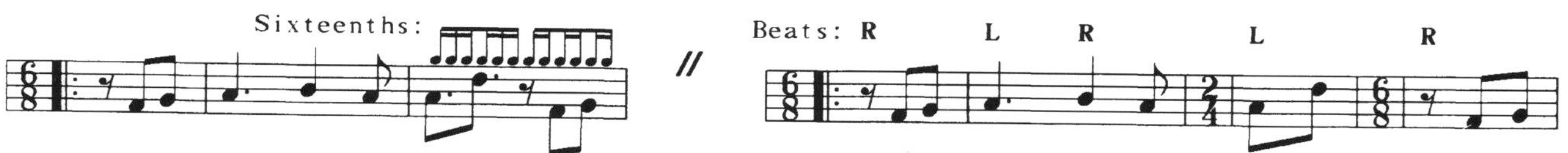

For drummers, this rhythm coincides with the first and last notes of a *Single Ratamacue*.

Here is Ostlings's transcription of 1939 which shows a different rhythm. No audio recordings survive for verification.

Harum Scarum
Fifer's Companion, 1805; traditionalized
Concert-Pitch Chords:
FIFE I
Walter D. Sweet
Fife-Pitch Chords:
FIFE II
Traditional
Snare DRUMS Bass
9-Stroke Rolloff
Snare DRUMS Bass
Pickup (as req'd)
First Full Measure of Tune

The strokes of the roll coincide with 32nd notes. The final roll consists of 49 strokes = (17-1) + (17-1) + 17

The Sailing Masters of 1812

Streetbeat

Used by permission

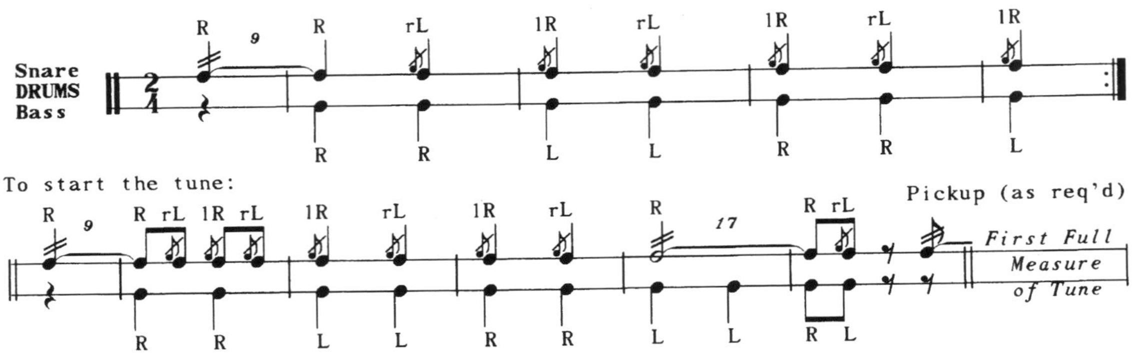
Snare
DRUMS
Bass
R 9 R rL lR rL lR rL lR
R R L L R R L
To start the tune:
R 9 R rL lR rL lR rL lR rL R 17 R rL
R R L L R R L L R L
Pickup (as req'd)
First Full Measure of Tune

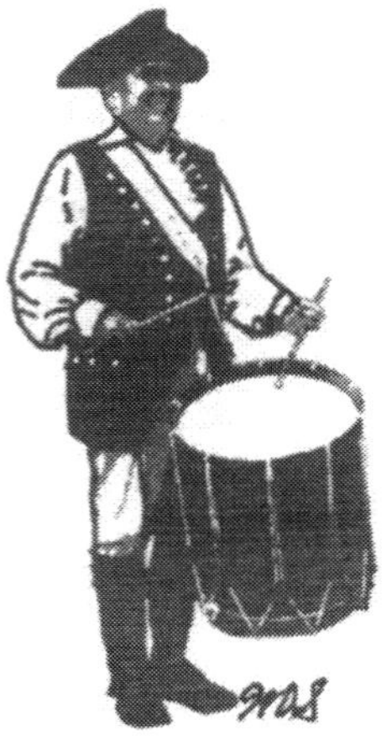

Starting a Tune with The Tapoff

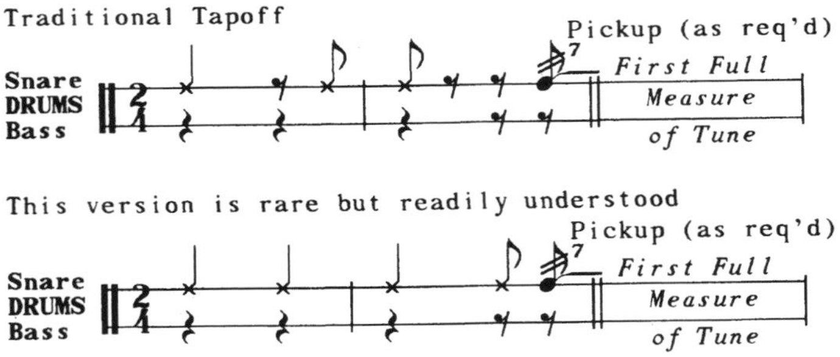
Traditional Tapoff
Snare
DRUMS
Bass
Pickup (as req'd)
First Full Measure of Tune
This version is rare but readily understood
Snare
DRUMS
Bass
Pickup (as req'd)
First Full Measure of Tune

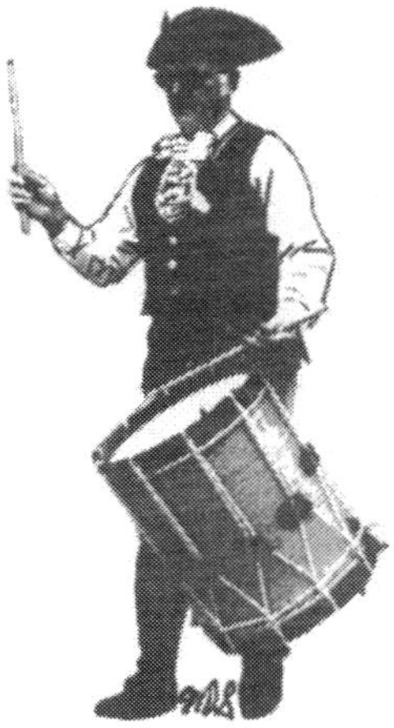

During the jam session, musicians stop playing between tunes. New starts are signaled by *The Tapoff*. The lead drummer strikes the rim (counterhoop) with a stick. *Tapoff* meter is always 2/4, even when the tune is in 6/8.

In some groups, one snare drummer will tap off, then pass the honor to the adjacent drummer for the next tune. In other groups, experience or pecking order indicates a lead drummer, who taps off all tunes until deposed.

Willie Weaver

Traditional

Concert-Pitch Chords:
FIFE I
D A7 D A7 D
A7 D A7 D D
A7 D A7 D

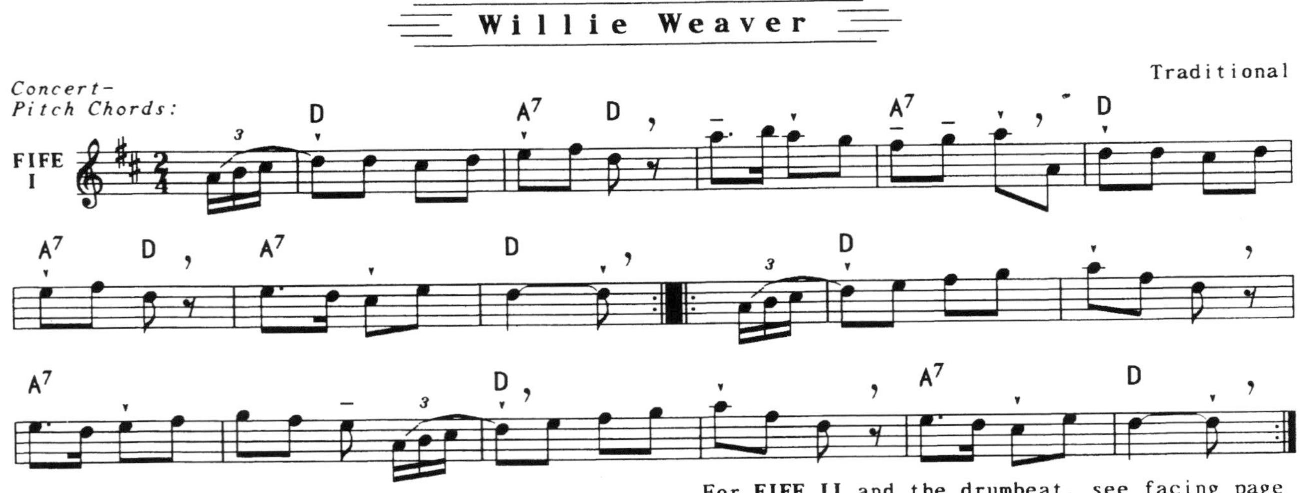

For FIFE II and the drumbeat, see facing page

Willie Weaver Continued

Crown Point

Roy Watrous, 1952
Used by permission

Concert-Pitch Chords:

FIFE I

D A7 D A7 D A7 D A7 D A7 A7 D A7 D A7 D A7 D A7 D

Walter D. Sweet

Fife-Pitch Chords:

FIFE II

B♭ F7 B♭ F7 B♭ F7 B♭ F7 B♭ F7 B♭ F7 B♭ F7 B♭ F7 B♭ F7 B♭

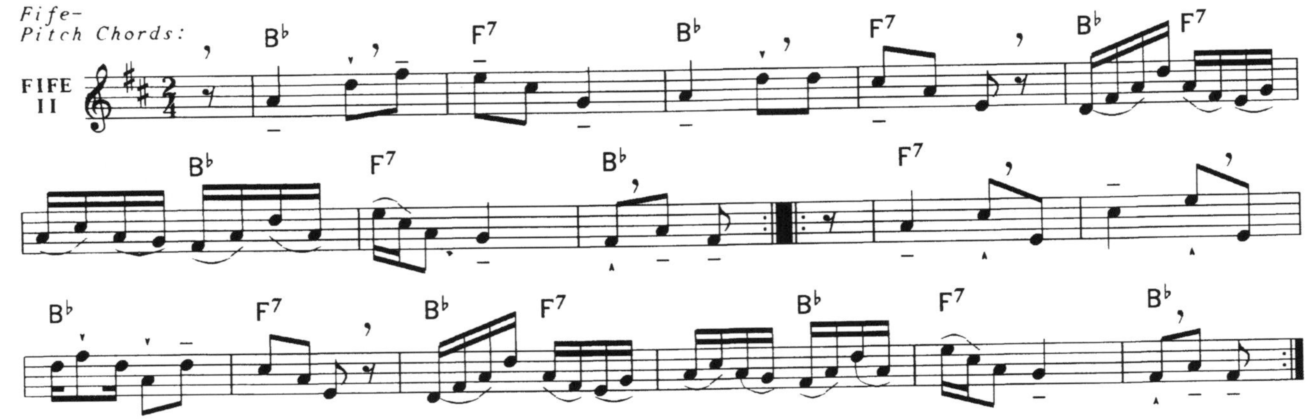

Dave Leroux and Bob Ward
Used by permission

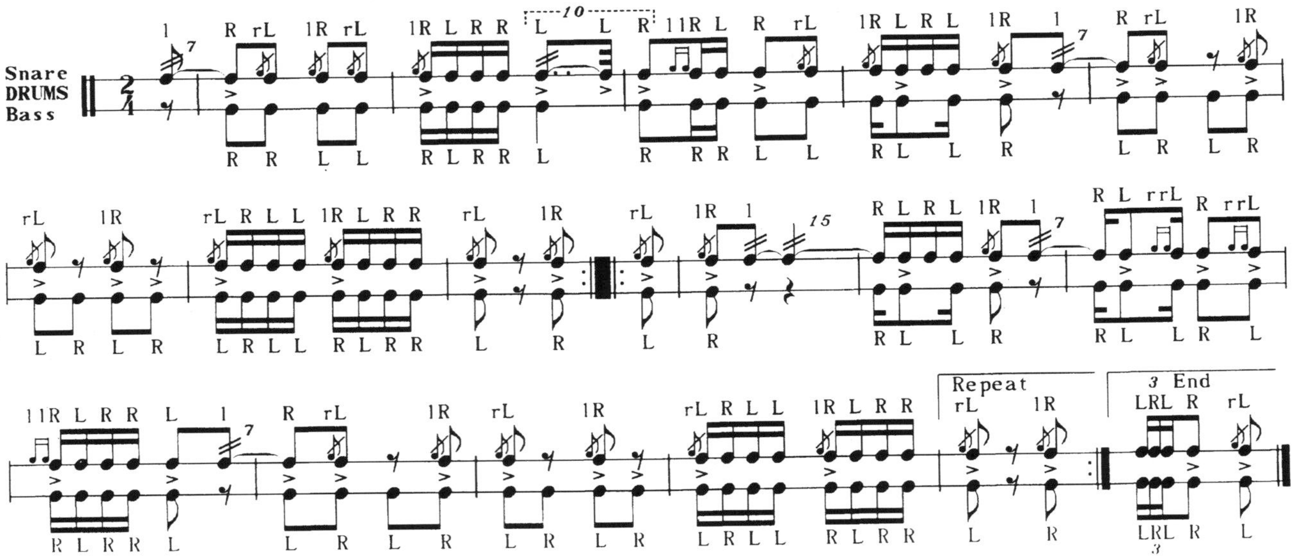

Snare DRUMS Bass

Repeat

3 End

Drums & Guns

Concert-Pitch Chords:
Roy Watrous, 1947
Used by permission
FIFE I
Fife-Pitch Chords:
Walter D. Sweet
FIFE II
Bob Ward
Used by permission
Snare
DRUMS
Bass
Measures at left are a variation of those directly above

Three Hundred Years

Hell on the Wabash

* Following the *Paradiddles*, Bruce & Emmett shows a *Ruff* ( ); this combination requires four consecutive strokes from one hand. In the author's opinion, only a *Flam* ( ) or a *Tap* ( ) is a reasonable follower at ♩=106. Hart's notations suspend the *Ruff* in corresponding figures.

Wrecker's Daughter

Conrad Fay, 1840; traditionalized

For the drumbeat, see facing page

Wrecker's Daughter Continued

Traditional

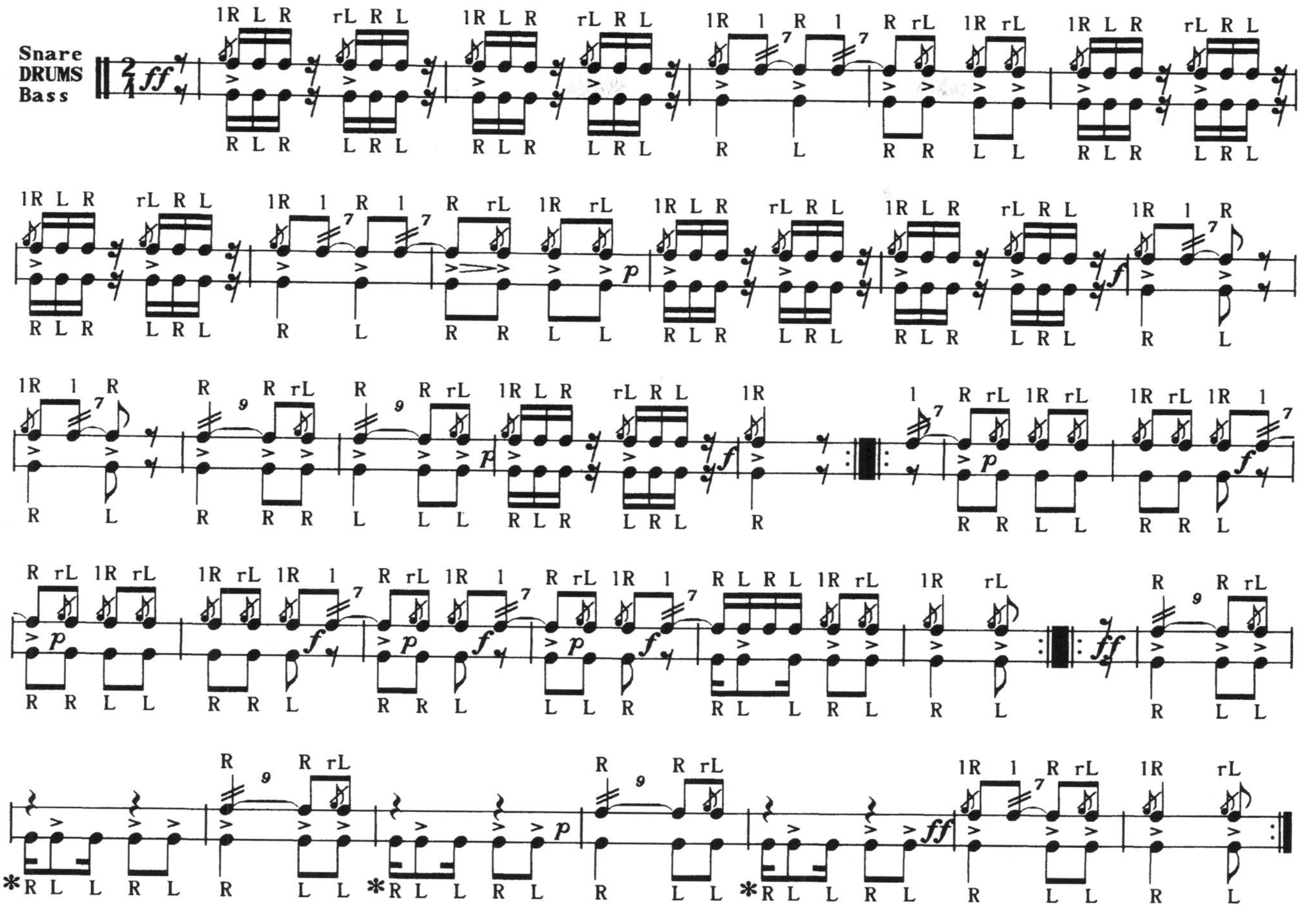

Snare
DRUMS
Bass

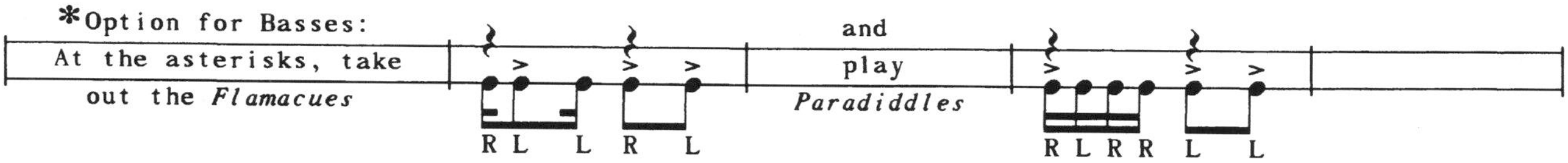

*Option for Basses: At the asterisks, take out the *Flamacues* and play *Paradiddles*

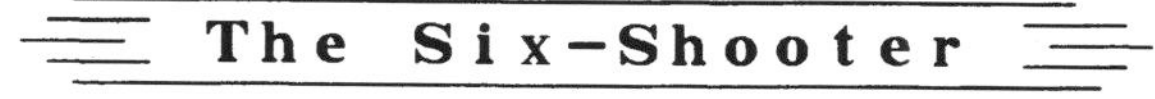

Streetbeat

Walter D. Sweet

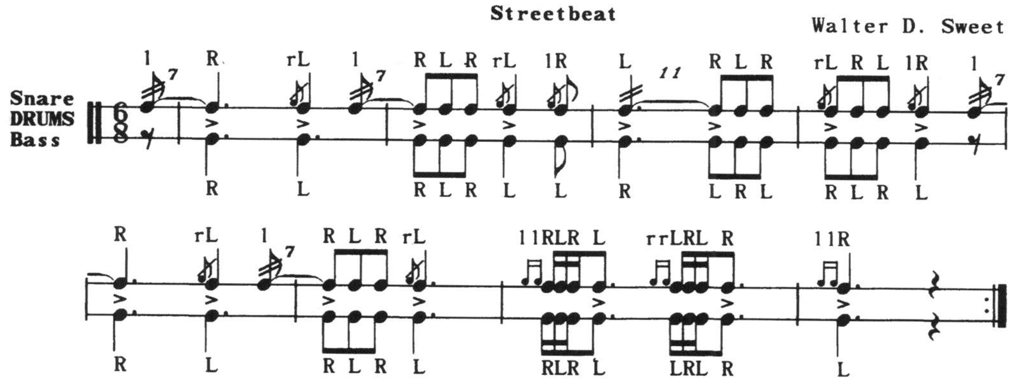

The Arkansas Traveler

The Northwest Passage

Turkey in the Straw

Turkey in the Straw
Continued

Traditional

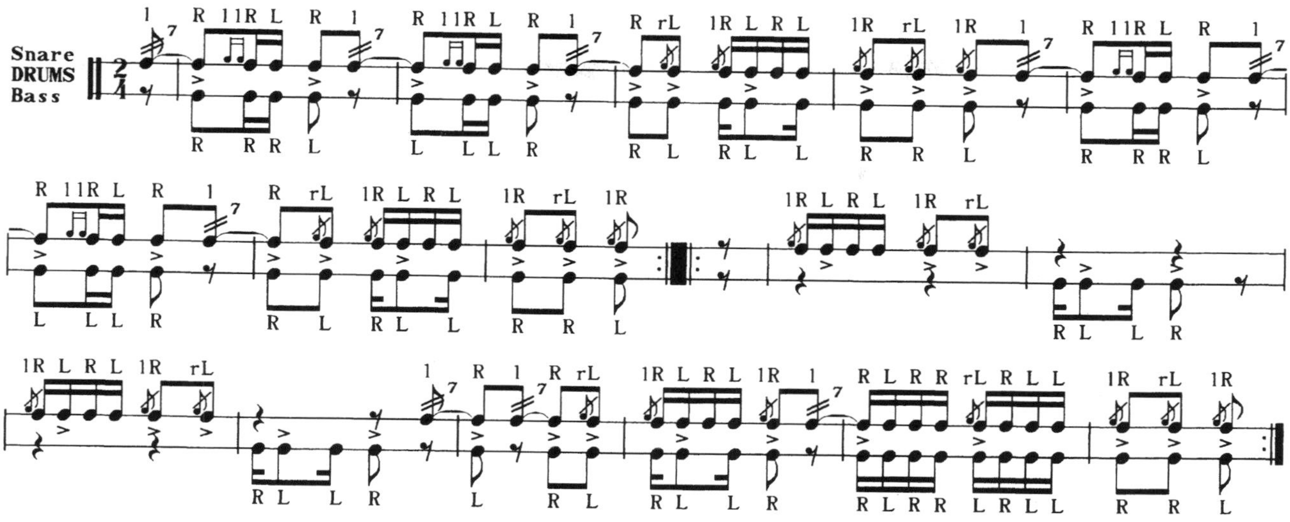

Snare
DRUMS
Bass

Fill

Traditional

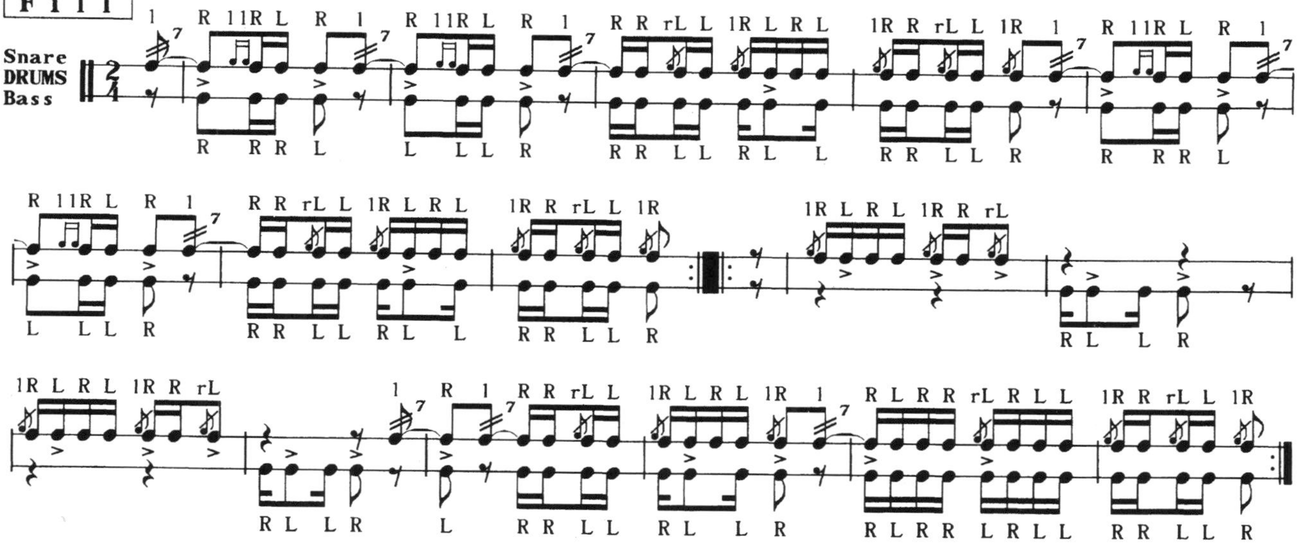

Snare
DRUMS
Bass

Shave-And-A-Haircut

Traditional ending

I
FIFES
II
Snare
DRUMS
Bass

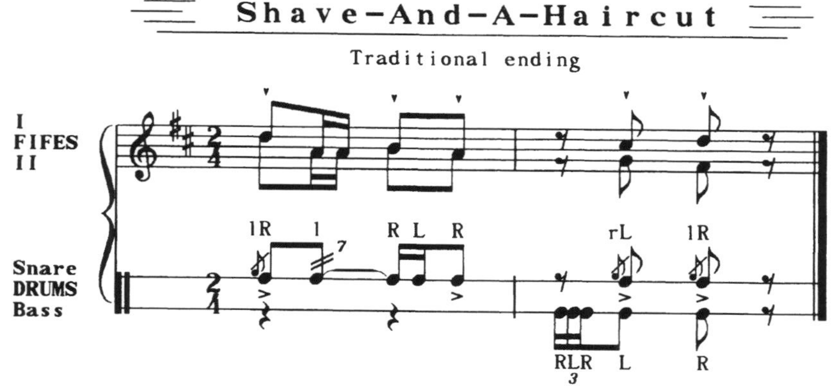

Katy Hill

Ostling, 1939

Concert-Pitch Chords:

FIFE I

G D7 G G D7 G D7 G

Walter D. Sweet

Fife-Pitch Chords:

FIFE II

E♭ B♭7 E♭ B♭7 E♭

*All these trills start on G (the upper note) and end on F# (the lower note). To ensure good effect, play at least 6 notes in the trill, then slur into the E and cut it short.

Ostling, 1939

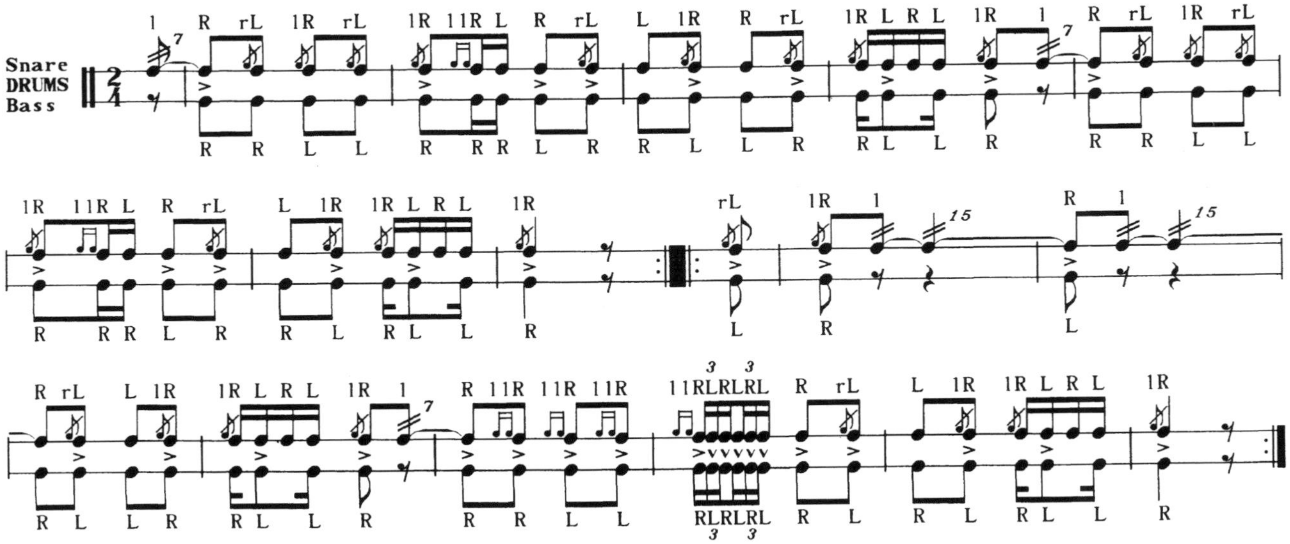

Snare DRUMS Bass

ROY'S RECYCLING

24-Hr Wrecker's Daughter Service

Dynamic Balancing

pp p mp mf f ff

Flats Fixed

High Beams Only

Staff Parking Only

Rest Area

Ruff Road Ahead

Nancy Hanks

Concert-Pitch Chords:
Traditional
FIFE I
Fife-Pitch Chords:
Walter D. Sweet
FIFE II
Dorence E. Smith, 1963
Snare DRUMS Bass

Cloverdale Jig

Traditional

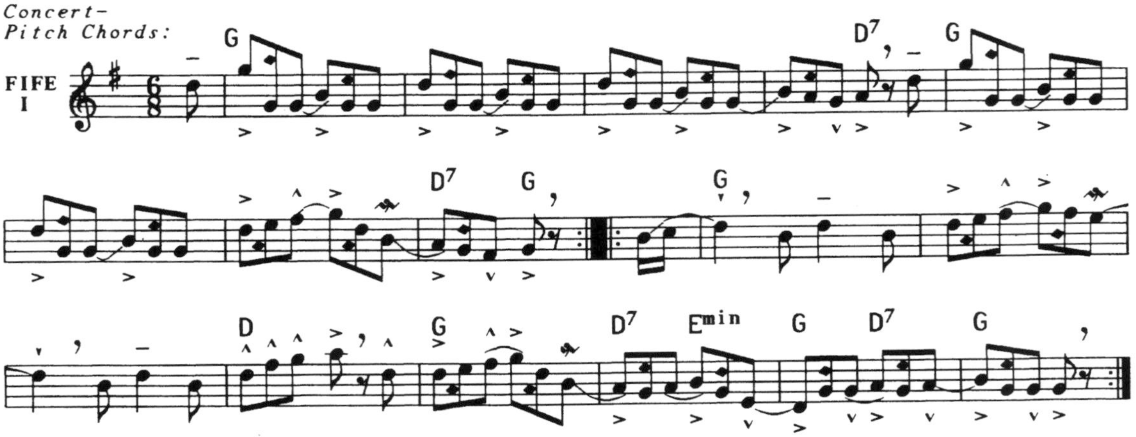

Concert-Pitch Chords:

G D7 G

D7 G G

D G D7 Emin G D7 G

FIFE I

Walter D. Sweet

Fife-Pitch Chords:

E♭ B♭7 E♭

B♭7 E♭ E♭

B♭ E♭ B♭7 Cmin E♭ B♭7 E♭

FIFE II

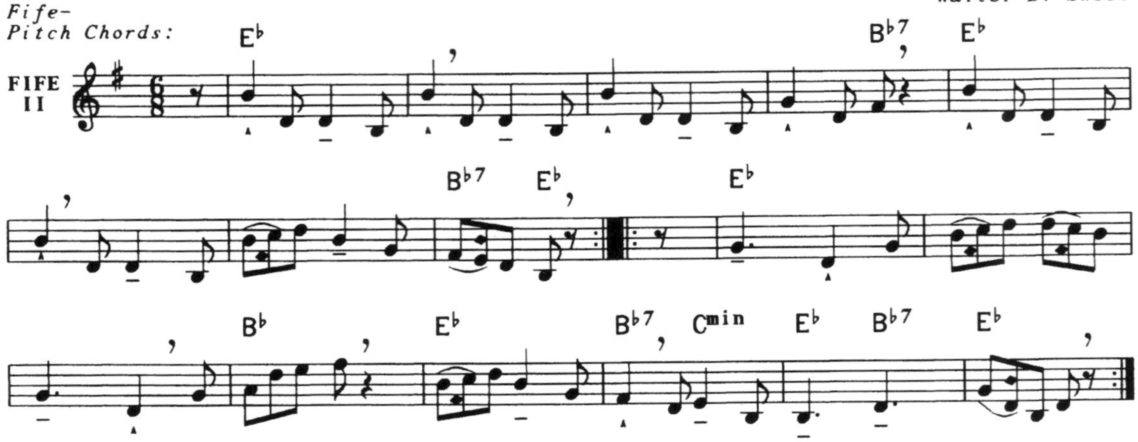

Traditional

Snare DRUMS Bass

Plain Six-Eight

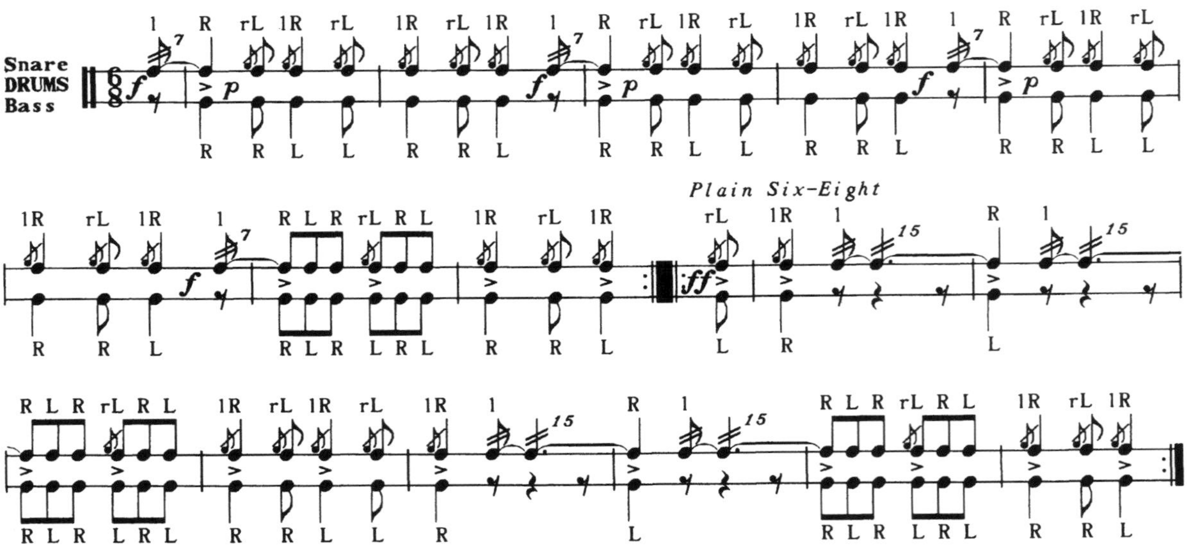

The Pet of the Pipers

*As necessary, omit these notes in order to breathe

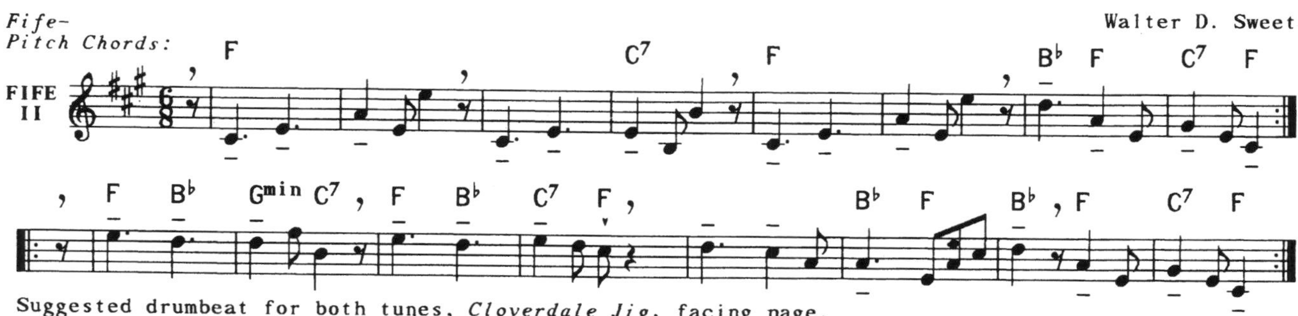

Suggested drumbeat for both tunes, *Cloverdale Jig*, facing page.

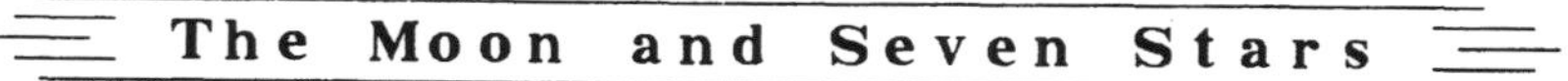

The Moon and Seven Stars

Granny, Will Your Dog Bite?

Pumpkin Creek

Chicken Reel

Traditional

Concert-Pitch Chords:

FIFE I — D, A7, D (X) … A7, D (Y) … D, A7, D … A7, D

At *, try substituting the measure at right. It distinguishes the middle of the phrase from the end.

Walter D. Sweet

Fife-Pitch Chords:

FIFE II — Bb, F7, Bb … Bb, F7, Bb

Play each strain four times.

For the drumbeat, see facing page.

See the Slow March, pp.78 & 79. Play from X to Y in 4/4 meter, ♩. ♪ rhythm.

One way of Ending a Tune

Many drummers use a flourish to end the music. One way is to play a *Single Seven* at the beginning of the last measure. Here are some applications:

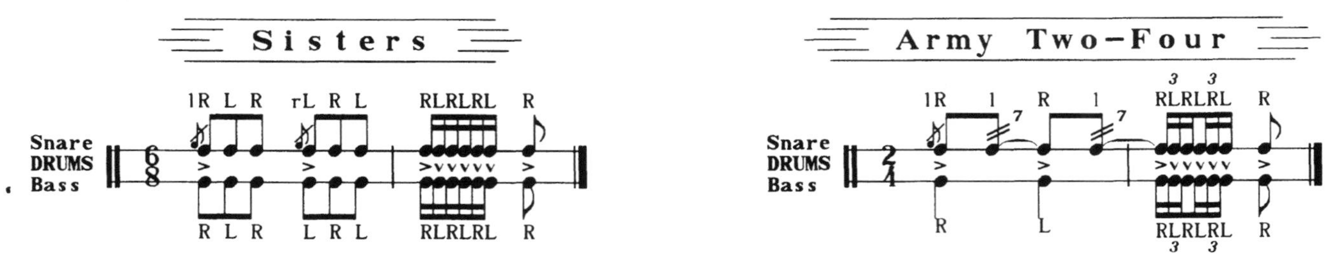

Chicken Reel Continued

Traditional

A

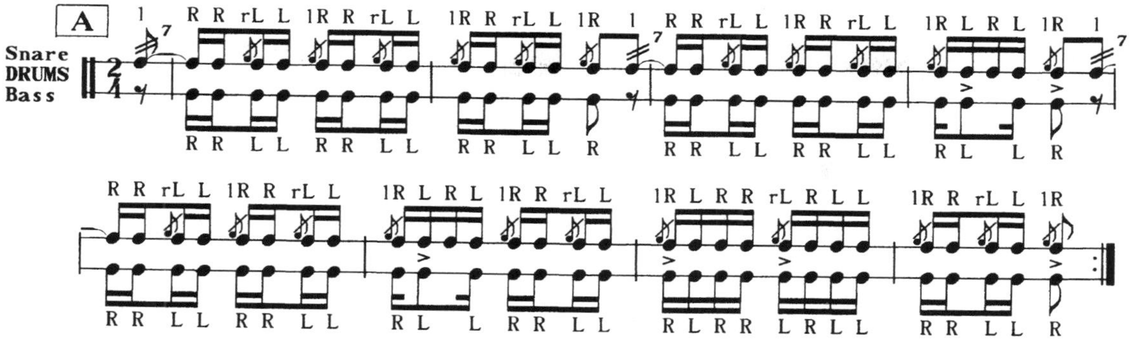

Snare DRUMS Bass

B

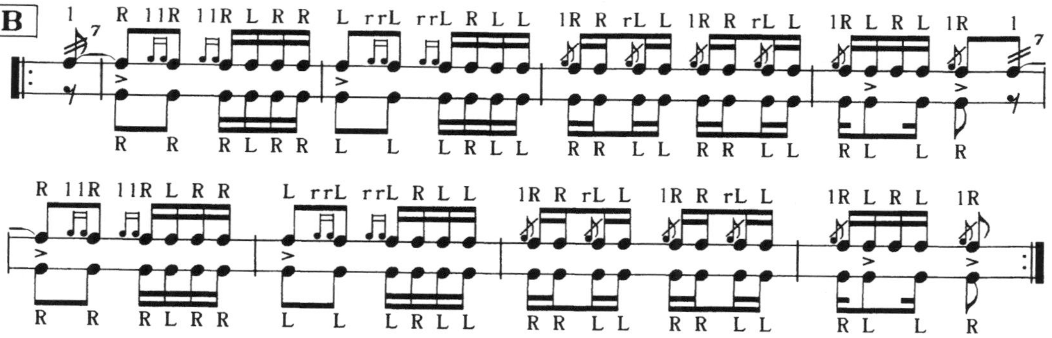

2nd Time

As played by Dorence E. Smith

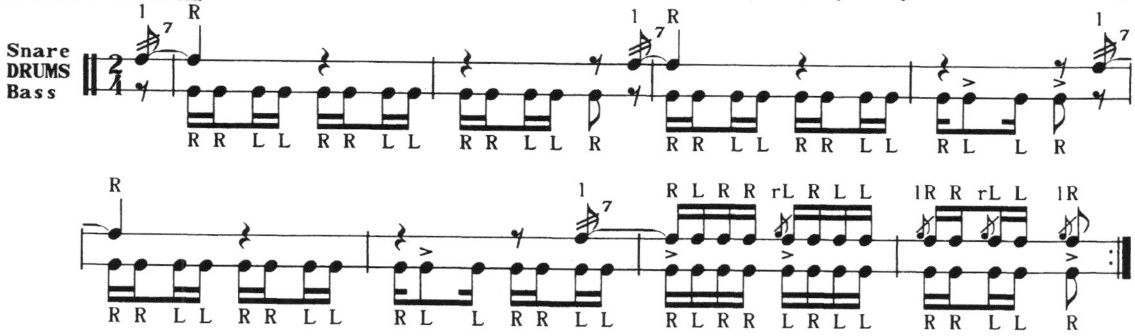

Snare DRUMS Bass

Snare drummers: during rests, point sticks straight up. After this, play B-strain, above.

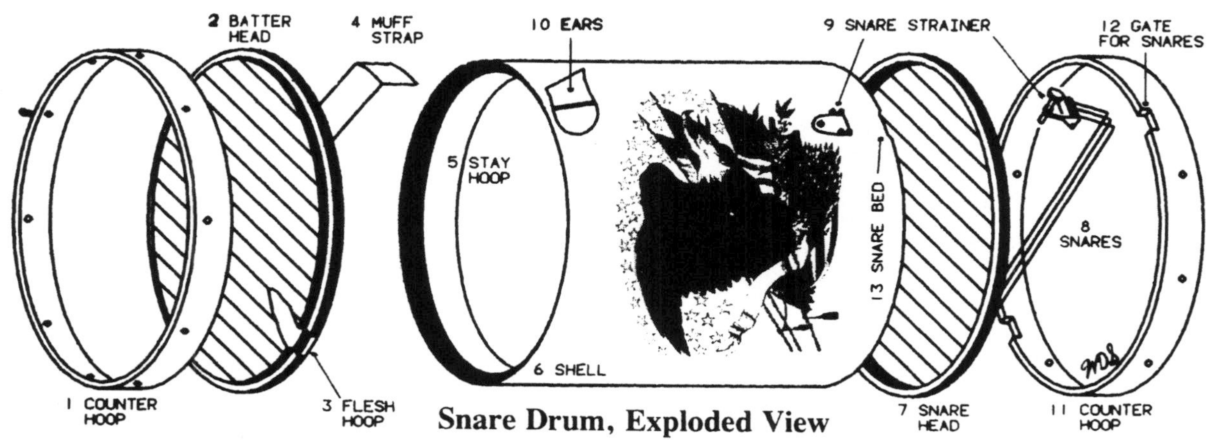

Snare Drum, Exploded View

The Tearful Drummer

♩=90

Do not drop the tempo below ♩=90. Remember, this is *music for the dead*, not *dead music*. In Bruce & Emmett, Snare-1 starts the B-strain with a tap in place of the rest; Snare-2 shall ". . . give the time to march by . . ."; all drums muffled. The author suggests one drummer to play Snare-2 on normal snares, while the others play Snare-1 muffled.

One way to do the

Slow March

First, consider a quickstep in 4/4 meter such as *Rally 'Round the Flag*. Here are the **footsteps** (L, R) corresponding to each **beat** (1, 2, 3, 4).
CONTINUED FACING PAGE.

4/4 | 1 L R 2 3 L R 4 | 1 L R 2 3 L R 4 |

Col. Robertson's Welcome

Concert-Pitch Chords: Emin D Emin B7 Emin G D Emin B7 Emin Emin D Emin B7 Emin G D Emin B7 Emin

Adapted from Bruce & Emmett 1862

FIFE I

Fife-Pitch Chords: Cmin B♭ Cmin G7 Cmin E♭ B♭ Cmin G7 Cmin Cmin B♭ Cmin G7 Cmin E♭ B♭ Cmin G7 Cmin

Walter D. Sweet

FIFE II

St. Patrick's Day in the Morning

James Clark

Used by permission

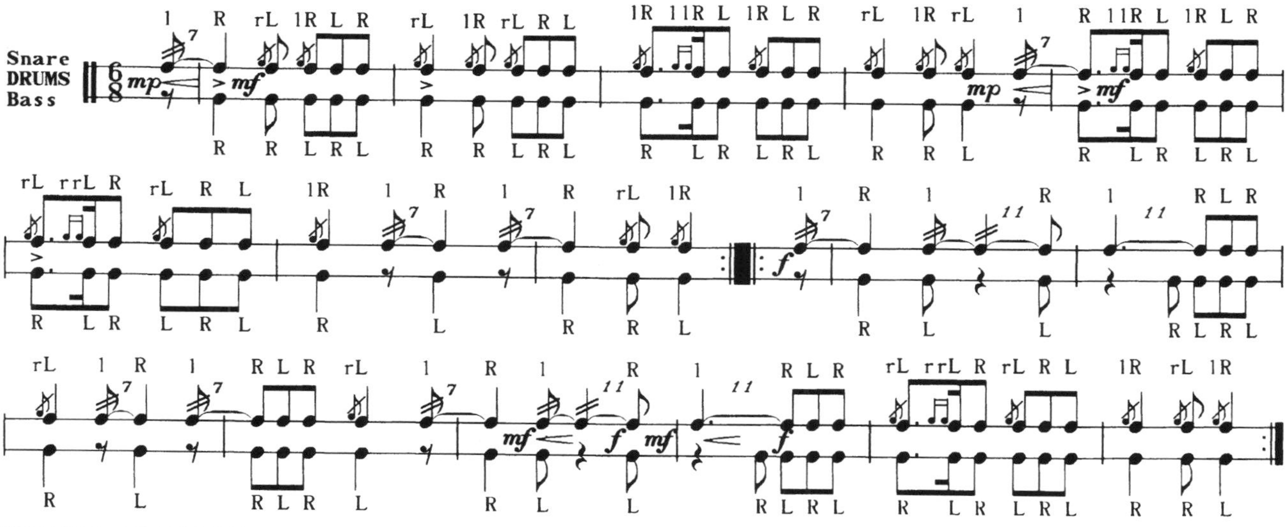

Snare DRUMS Bass

For the Slow March, step Left on beat 1. Then, on beat 2, move the right foot forward, but don't set it down: instead, let it hang in front, level, 2" above the ground. On beat 3, drop the right foot straight down. In the 2nd example, note beats 2 and 3, the symbol for "hang and drop" and the complete pattern. Here are some tunes to try with the Slow March:

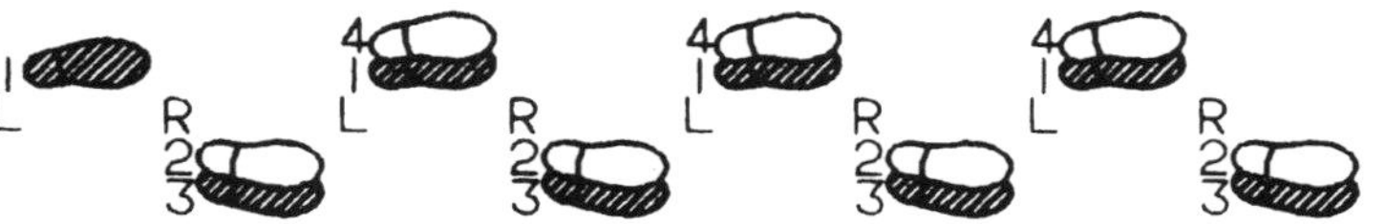

Blue & The Gray 9 ◆ Just Before the Battle 17 ◆ Tramp! Tramp! Tramp! 21 ☐ See pp. 24 & 76; Slow March from X to Y in common time, then D.C. in cut time for a quickstep as written.

Snare Drum, Sectional View
For legend, see page 77

A general-purpose drumbeat

The General

Traditional

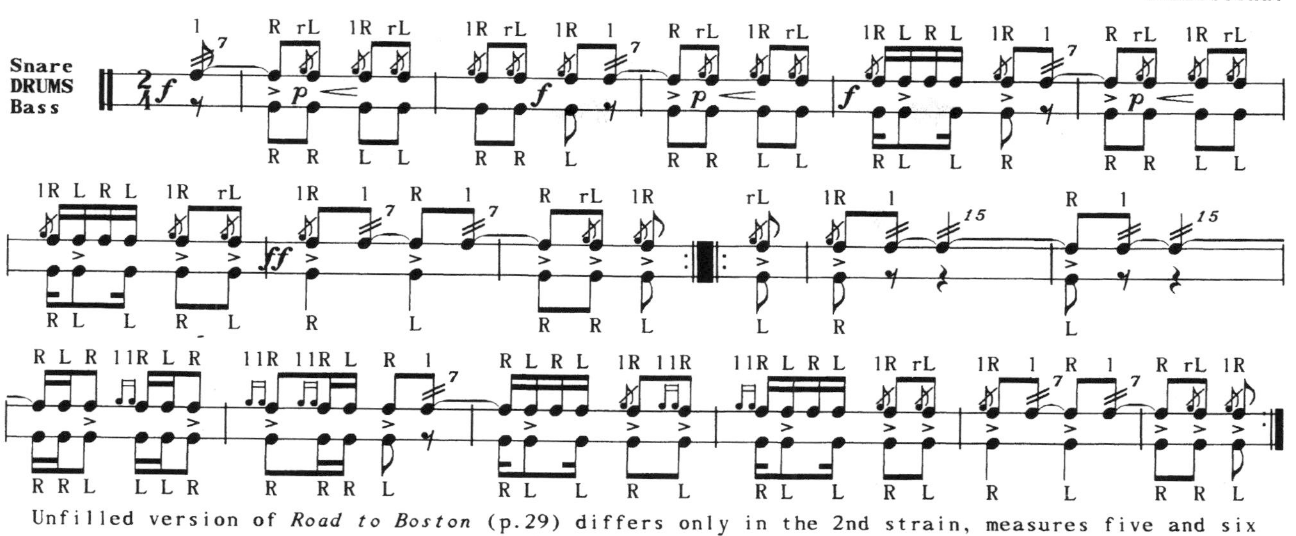

Unfilled version of *Road to Boston* (p.29) differs only in the 2nd strain, measures five and six

Fill

Traditional

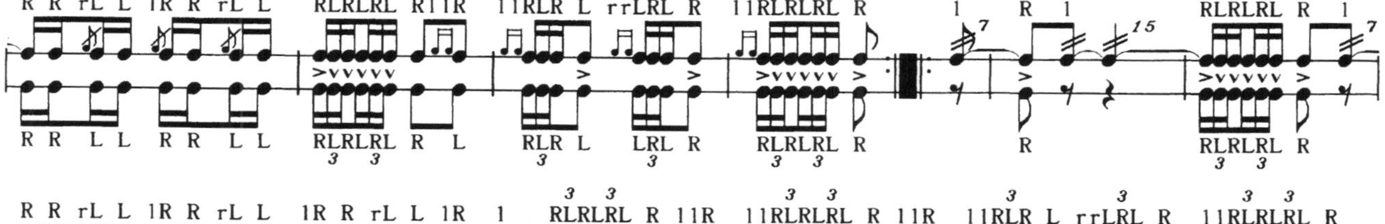

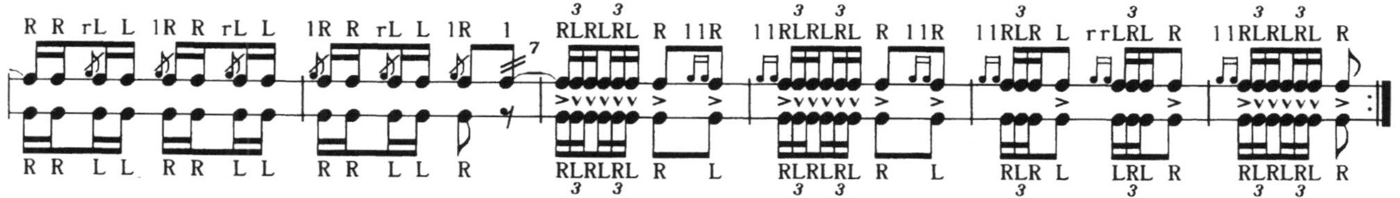

Nutmeg Volunteers

Streetbeat

Used by permission

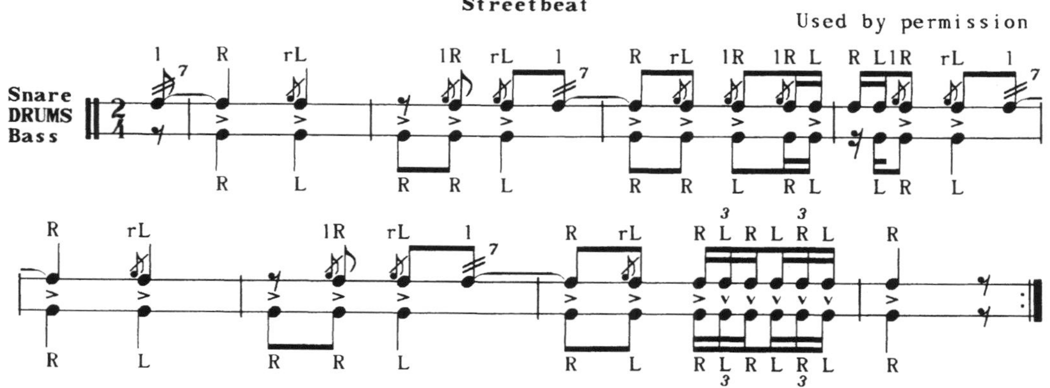

Pig Town Fling

Inimitable

Concert-Pitch Chords:
Traditional
FIFE I
D G D A7
D G D A7 D
G D7
G D7 G
Fife-Pitch Chords:
Walter D. Sweet
FIFE II
B♭ E♭ B♭ F7 B♭ E♭
B♭ F7 B♭ E♭
B♭7 E♭ B♭7 E♭
Dorence E. Smith, 1981
Snare DRUMS Bass

Scotty O'Neil
Bob McQuillen, 1972
Used by permission
Concert-Pitch Chords:
FIFE I
Walter D. Sweet
Fife-Pitch Chords:
FIFE II
Dorence E. Smith, 1981
Snare DRUMS Bass
Learner's Streetbeat
Snare DRUMS Bass

The Haversack

The Star-Spangled Banner

♩=90

Bar lines are re-assigned to reflect the fermatas: held notes are three beats each.

Fifing

How is it that two musicians can play from the same notation, yet sound different? The answer is a matter of style.

Fifing styles are numerous. In terms of style, one fifer will have much in common with another fifer, and little in common with a concert flautist, for example. In this book, the transcriptions reflect one particular fifing style which is not universal, but it is characteristic.

The chief elements of style are phrasing, syncopation, dynamics, articulation, accenting, and ornaments. The particular combination of these elements, to a particular degree, comprises one style.

Phrasing Fifing aims to rouse, rather than soothe. Short phrasing lets fifers breathe, which provides for loudness and contrast. In *Yankee Doodle*, phrases are mostly two bars long; this is typical of traditional fifing. *Drums and Guns* is very demanding in terms of phrasing. *Cincinnati Hornpipe* and *President Garfield's Hornpipe* have many notes in long phrases which preclude other stylistic expression.

Syncopation commonly appears in 6/8 meter, where triplets repeat. The first note is lengthened, while the second is shortened to create "swing". The following transcription⇨ is excessive; a milder timeshift would be written as or *schematically*

Dynamics Fife and drum corps provide field music, not chamber music. Therefore, fifers are expected to play loud, not soft. Fifes are naturally louder on the high notes. Dynamics is the dominion of drummers; fifers follow.

Articulation Tonguing and slurring interplay on a very small scale. Sound and silence are both musical elements. *Shave-And-A-Haircut* focuses on silence. This motif is echoed in *Pumpkin Creek* at the end of the first strain.

Refer to the transcription below. Have player #1 play passage A (slurred). Now add player #2 on passage B (staccato). Both players start each note simultaneously. B ends each note earlier than its face value: this is the functional definition of staccato. Therefore, C means D, not E. The slur suspends tonguing between notes. The last note has no follower in the group; its time of ending is not dictated by the slur.

A

B

C

D

E

CONTRADICTORY

"Slur to staccato" is controversial; perhaps the issue is not the transcription but the appeal it has for a given listener.

This pattern has been applied to the tunes in this book. Examples: in *The Green Cockade*, where the melody has peaks and troughs; in *Pumpkin Creek,* at the first of repeated notes.

Accenting is prominent in 6/8 meter, where triplets repeat (see *Paddy O'Toole*). Some tunes in 2/4 meter have pedal points

or filler notes. In these cases, the principal notes merit accents (see *Drums and Guns*). Fifing accents do not necessarily coincide with drumming accents.

Ornaments The most common ornament is the triplet run from Sol to Do (see *Yankee Doodle* and *Hell on the Wabash*). Where the fingering is clumsy, the device is not applied (*Finnegan's Wake*, second strain, beginning).

Trills are often used to break up sustained notes or establish a counterpoint (see *Some Distance from Prussia*).

Bruce & Emmett shows turns in certain tunes. The device is not used by traditional fifers as a stylistic option.

Grace notes have more effect when playing solo than ensemble. In one sense, a staccato note which follows a slur functions as a final grace note (see example C on the previous page).

In summary, style is a set of habits which outweigh the notation. Traditional musicians acquire style by osmosis in the course of learning tunes.

Beyond the scope of this book, style is measured subjectively: a decoration in one style is a blemish in another. Style is one of many criteria for measuring excellence.

Accord It is a fifer's job to impart excitement by means of clarity, loudness, and expression. Occasionally, the excitement outstrips the attention to playing in tune. However, deliberate dissonance is neither pretty nor authentic. Quality of music and pride in performance are just as valid today as in years past. Bear in mind that the following combinations of fifes often clash: old and new; prestigious and commonplace; tapered bore and straight bore. Tuning one note will not bring divergent scales into accordance. For corps playing, choose a fife for its ability to play in tune with the others.

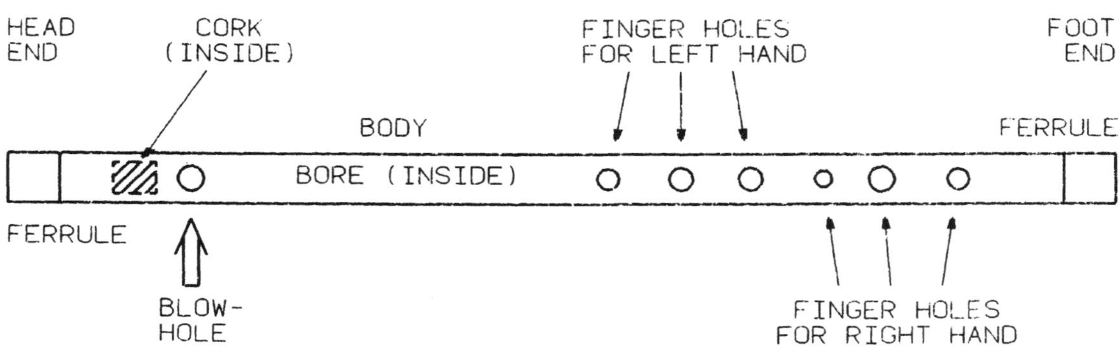

Rudimental Drumming

Rudimental drumming is a discipline based on subroutines or building blocks. Each rudiment is an entity of strokes, rhythm, loudness, and sticking. Without rudiments, drummers are unable to work as a team, to increase the loudness while maintaining artistic expression. Rudimental drumming helped historic drummers to be heard on the battlefield; the practice is equally effective in the firemen's parade. Bass drummers also use rudiments. See page vi, **Implied Understandings**, for a partial explanation.

The art of traditional drumming includes practices not always evident in print. *Connecticut Halftime* has a very simple notation. In a **closed style** of drumming, these 7-stroke rolls occur strictly as written:

However, a traditional drummer will play this familiar piece in an **open style**, which could be notated as follows:

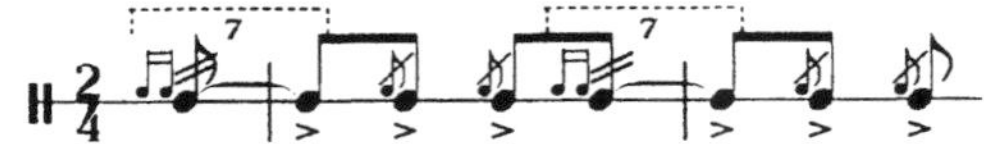

The rolls will start early and take more time than the allotted eighth note (seven slower strokes). If the early start resets the metronome in the listener's mind, and the rolls take longer, then the drum part is perceived as lagging behind the beat. However, to a traditional drummer, the open style is essential and natural. Openness varies. Exactly *how open* and *where* are matters of taste for a drummer playing alone; for ensemble playing, all drummers must agree.

In the recording that accompanies this book, the drummer plays in an open style, especially the 7-stroke pickup rolls. In 6/8 meter, the pickup rolls are opened well in excess of the written eighth note; sometimes they sound the same as pickup rolls in 2/4 meter. Some traditional drummers play much more open than the musicians on this recording.

The open style of drumming has been in use since before the Civil War. Hart's Instructor (1862) discusses the open and closed style. Bruce and Emmett (1862) on page 13, insists on the closed style: "The performer should never *hurry* or *drag* the time . . . [but rather] . . .beat his rolls as close as possible . . . [thus] . . . the 'rest' between the strokes will consequently be longer."

Sticking is the assignment of each drum stroke to the left or right hand.

Dynamics and sticking are interrelated. To demonstrate, use one stick to play a series of loud eighth notes. After each stroke, the hand raises the stick in preparation for the next. Now play sixteenth notes. The hand has not as much time to raise the stick. As a result, each note is not as loud as before. Continue playing sixteenths with one hand. On the first beat of every four, add a stroke from the other hand. This new combined stroke will be naturally louder.

Consider successive *Paradiddles*. Conventional sticking is ⇩

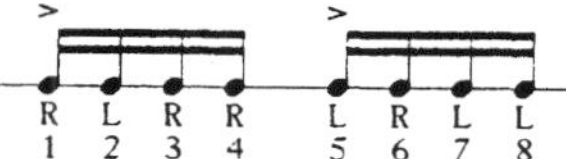

Note strokes 3 4 5 6. While the right hand repeats, the left hand has ample time to prepare a strong stroke #5. By design, strokes 3 4 and 6 keep a soft contrast by repeating the action of the right hand. The sticking and the accenting work together.

The **Drum Fill** is a companion version of the drumbeat. Like "theme and variation," the Fill is fancier and more difficult, though largely compatible with the Straight version. When artfully executed, drum fills are the test of a drummer's mettle, a point of pride for the corps, and a motivator for the aspiring drummer.

Fills follow a recipe, based on traditional rules. For example, *Connecticut Halftime* consists of four strains. For the first filling, change the ending of each phrase to a *Single Seven*. For the second filling, add this: substitute *Single Ratamacues* for every *Paradiddle*.

Repeated Drumbeats. Many corps have a "default" drumbeat. In Bruce & Emmett, *Army 2/4* is assigned to *Biddy Oats* and 13 other tunes. In other corps, *Connecticut Halftime* is equally common.

Rudimental Transcription Written music is divided into measures and beats. Some rudiments overlap these arbitrary boundaries. The *15-Stroke Roll* occupies 1½ beats. Transcription⇨ supports the division of beats. The same phrase transcribed as⇨ supports the integrity of the rudiment. Likewise, one-beat rudiments are difficult to recognize when split. Consider Connecticut Halftime, line 2.⇨ is conventional, but⇨ clearly shows the *Lesson-25* in the middle. See *Pig Town Fling*, strain 2, measure 1. In conventional notation, rudimental execution depends on rudiment names, accent marks and sticking marks.

Oldness alone does not constitute tradition. Modern English has its own traditions, and little regard for Shakespeare's. When practices fall into disuse, they cease to be traditional. To play out obsolete practices is reenactment. In 1960, *York Fusiliers* was passé; it has become popular with this generation, and is now traditional (it has been revived). *The Road to Boston* is a traditional tune, played from 1776 thru today (it has survived). *Drums & Guns* (1947) is recent, but it has the style and popularity of old favorites.

Tradition perpetuates the music, but subjects it to change. When scholars re-introduce historic music, it will be changed by players as it becomes traditional music. Sometimes, a traditional tune remains stable for years, e.g., *The Road to Boston*. Usually, a tune changes in these ways:

Melodies are simplified or embellished *Yankee Doodle* changed from 1777 (Gibbs ms) to 1862 (Bruce & Emmett), and continues to change. *Grandfather's Clock* has been published widely since (1876), but fifers insists on their own version. Runs and trills have been added to *The Girl I Left Behind Me*.

Meter changes *Reel of Stumpie* (2/4) is the predecessor of *Sisters* (6/8). *Grandfather's Clock,* originally in 4/4, is now played in cut time. Fifers now experiment with *Eighteen-Twelve*, and change the meter from 2/4 to 6/8.

Phrases outlive tunes Old cars go to the junkyard to be dismantled. Parts are stored for reuse. Similarly, when tunes fall into disuse, their phrases sometimes separate. The phrases lie dormant in our musical subconscious, later to be recombined as "new" tunes. This is not plagiarism, but traditional music's recycling program! *The Rakes of Mallow* makes up the second strain of *Irish Reel*.

The non-musical details change *Paddy O'Toole* is also known as *The Power of Whiskey*. Legends have sprung up around a few special tunes, e.g., *Garry Owen*. For some tunes, their origin is a mystery, e.g., *Old Saybrook*. Sometimes an anonymous tune falls into disuse, only to reappear with credit to an identifiable composer, e.g., *Village Quickstep*.

In traditional music, change is slow. Music introduced today may become popular, but to be adopted, usually takes a generation. This principle applies to new music as well as to the products of research. The American Bicentennial impelled the resurrection of manuscripts from colonial times; only some of this old music was adopted by today's musicians. Fife and drum music is not revolutionary: it is evolutionary.

Tradition perpetuates performance practices, too. Characteristic practices are rudimental drumming, and fifing which uses "slur to staccato." This combination is called, "Ancient Fifing and Drumming" to distinguish it from modern corps whose players observe classical conventions. For further explanation, see **Traditional Playing Style**, page 87.

Tradition has no loyalty for sources of tunes. *Wrecker's Daughter* was a sentimental song. *Rally 'Round the Flag* was patriotic. *Turkey in the Straw* was a minstrel song. *Chester* was a hymn. *The Northwest Passage* was taken from the sound track of the movie. Fifers have heard *Rondeau* on television. Yes, some fife tunes were military airs; others were dance tunes.

Music changes anywhere, anytime. Fifers and drummers regularly improvise at jam sessions. Ed Olsen forgot half a tune on his way home from the theater (see *Northwest Passage*). The conventions of notation have changed in 200 years, leaving old manuscripts open to new interpretation. Errors in notation are propagated. Some music is learned from old-timers, whose arthritis simplifies many tunes.

In summary, traditional fifing and drumming is a folk activity, perpetuated and altered by the players. It is a mix of tunes from many sources, and responds to the influences of the day. It is characterized by performance practices including rudimental drumming, and "slur to staccato" (among fifers). Some tunes and drumbeats have a rich history, while others are obscure.

Histories of the Tunes and Drumbeats

by Susan L. Cifaldi

In preparing these notes, I am indebted to the work of several fine scholars. Acton Ostling, formerly a drummer with the Chester Fife and Drum Corps, began the real work of collecting and documenting music of Connecticut's traditional fife and drum corps back in the 1930s. His Music of '76 (1939) preserves some of this music. This book plus Ostling's papers at The Company of Fifers and Drummers library are a rich source of early twentieth-century Connecticut tradition. Another excellent regional study was prepared by Samuel P. Bayard, Dance to the Fiddle, March to the Fife (1980). Bayard began collecting tunes from fifers and fiddlers in the West Virginia / Western Pennsylvania area in 1928. The Company of Fifers and Drummers solicited popular tunes from Connecticut Valley corps just before the Bicentennial and published their collections in two volumes, known to many simply as the Company Books. Their real value may be the large number of drumbeats they contain. The National Tune Index, Part I (Kate Van Winkle Keller and Carolyn Rabson, 1980) and the National Tune Index, Part II (Raoul F. Camus, 1989) is a comprehensive bibliography of more than 50,000 secular tunes c. 1636-1836, an indispensable tool for tracing early tune histories. Another valuable resource, although not yet in print (!), is Ed Olsen, Archivist for The Company of Fifers and Drummers, whose devotion to fife and drum tradition is matched only by his dynamic efforts to preserve it.

Ancient & Honorable Artillery The drumbeat and an accompanying tune are found in Bruce and Emmett's Drummer's and Fifer's Guide (1862), hereafter called B & E. The title may refer to Boston's Ancient & Honourable Artillery Company.

Arkansas Traveler The first known printing of this jaunty melody was in 1847. The famous dialog story appeared in sheet music printed sometime near the beginning of the Civil War, and was illustrated by Currier and Ives in 1870. -K.K.

Army Six-Eight B & E (1862) applies this drumbeat to *The Corkonian* and nine other tunes. A general-purpose drumbeat.

Army Two-Four B & E (1862) applies this drumbeat to *Biddy Oats* and 13 other tunes. It is an old favorite, and always handy in the absence of a drumbeat tailored to the tune.

Battle Hymn of the Republic Lyrics written by Julia Ward Howe in 1861 established the title and reputation of this hymn turned political tune. An earlier set of lyrics, *John Brown's Body*, is described by Vera Brodsky Lawrence as a "lighthearted spoof" of a Massachusetts sergeant which "took off like the proverbial wildfire" and soon came to represent the John Brown of Harper's Ferry fame. Earlier still is a hymn called *Glory Hallelujah*. *Battle Hymn* is sometimes coupled with *When Johnny Comes Marching Home* as a medley.

Blackberry Quadrille appears in Don Messer's Way Down East Fiddlin' Tunes (1948).

Blue and the Gray. Words and music were written after 1900 by Paul Dresser, the elder brother of novelist Theodore Dreiser. The Spanish-American War inspired patriotic sentiment about the Civil War, and many new songs after the fact. The first line gives an alternate title and the theme: *A Mother's Gift to Her Country* (i.e., the sacrifice of her sons in war). **FIFE II** has 3 patriotic counter-melodies, as in old arrangements. -W.D.S.

Bonnie Blue Flag is one of the few known Confederate tunes played by traditional fifers. Lyrics were written by Harry McCarthy in the 1860s.

British Grenadiers. Ramsay cites lyrics from 1759 in praise of the elite British soldiers of the grenadier regiments. This tune appears earlier as a ballad, *All You That Love Good Fellows*. -K.K.

Caledonia This tune is preserved with the title *My Love She Is* in several fife manuscripts of the 1780s. It is found in the tradition as *Caledonia*. The tune *Ivoryton No. 1*, listed on a Deep River Drum Corps repertory sheet c. 1900, has been identified as *My Love She Is* by Ed Olsen who further speculates that it had been a street tune from the old Ivoryton Drum Corps. Bayard found 22 versions of the tune in Pennsylvania tradition between 1930 and 1960 and called it "possibly...the best known instrumental folk tune" that he had found. A drumbeat for *My Love / Caledonia* appears in Benjamin Clark's manuscript (1799) and in Levi Lovering's Drummer's Assistant (1819).

Chicken Reel was published in 1910 by Joseph Daly, who claimed to have composed it. It was billed as a "Performer's Buck," i.e., music for a snappy tap dance. Fans of Bugs Bunny hear this tune when Foghorn Leghorn appears on screen.

City Guards. The first strain appears in Riley's Flute Melodies as *Miss Ray's Fancy* (vol. 1, 1814), then as *Rustic Reel* (vol. 4, c.1826), a common title. Bayard collected this tune as *Oh, Dear Mother, My Toes Are Sore,* noting stability of the first strain, and variety of the second. -K.K.

Cloverdale Jig comes from the repertoire of the Warehouse Point Corps. In structure, the melody is reminiscently Irish, although no source is known. The drumbeat is simple, effective, and adaptable. -W.D.S.

Col. Robertson's Welcome appears in B & E (1862) on page 61.

Columbia, the Gem of the Ocean was copyrighted in 1843 by a Philadelphia publisher, composition credited to David T. Shaw. Also called, *The Red, White and Blue* from its lyrics. -K.K.

Connecticut Halftime is also known as *Halftime* or *Old Halftime* Without the fills (variations), it was published in Hart's Instructor for the Drum (1862) to accompany *Rosebud Reel*. This drumbeat fits most tunes in 2/4 or 4/4 meter. Note that the musical phrase is 4 measures: **half** the usual length. Many drumbeats have "*Halftime*" in the title.

Crown Point was written by Roy Watrous in 1952. The title refers to the New York fort which played a significant part in the French & Indian War and in the Revolutionary War. Watrous wrote the tune after the drumbeat by Bob Ward (Hubert Ablondi).

Roy Watrous began composing in 1947. He once fifed with the Sons of Liberty; he co-founded the Ancient Mariners in 1959.

Dan Tucker See *Old Dan Tucker*.

Dixie immediately established the reputation of its composer, Daniel Decatur Emmett. It was published shortly after its first performance, 4 April 1859. A minstrel song, *Dixie* soon acquired political symbolism for the South during the Civil War, even though it was popular in the North at that time. A "walkaround" strain is included in B & E, but not here. While the walkaround was an important part of the minstrel performance, it is not usually played by traditional fifers and drummers.

Downfall of Paris appears in the manuscript tune collection begun by Massachusetts fifer Abel Shattuck about 1801. By the 1860s it had become a staple in the fife literature and was published in B & E (1862). Although the first measure of *Ah, Ça Ira* is the same as the first measure of *Downfall*, they are different tunes.

Drums and Guns was written by Roy Watrous in 1947. The title is a phrase which recurs in the ballad *Johnny Has Gone for a Soldier*. The drumbeat was written by Bob Ward (Hubert Ablondi).

Eighteen-Twelve This tune began in the 1700s as *Welcome Here Again*. *Welcome* was used as a fifer's march early in the

Revolutionary War, a tradition which continued well into the next two centuries. The changes which occurred over the years resulted in a "new" tune, *Eighteen-Twelve*. Despite the title, there is no evidence that *Eighteen-Twelve* was played by fifers during the War of 1812. The tune does not turn up with that title or in that form in any of the surviving period literature, printed or manuscript, until 1888 when it was printed as *Morrisville* in the American Fife Instructor. In 1905, it appears as *Eighteen-Twelve* in American Veteran Fifer, hereafter called AVF.

Essence of Tampa Composition is credited to Sam Goodman. Sam once fifed with the Steeplechase Drum Corps of Coney Island, NY and later with the 71st Regiment.

Fancy Six-Eight is a general-purpose drumbeat. Compare it to *Plain Six-Eight*.

Father O'Flynn This jig appears in Aird's third Selection (1788) as *The Top of Cork Road*.

Fifty Cents Ed Olsen recalls first hearing this tune played by the Veteran Corps of Artillery, whose field music was added in the early 1900s. Later, Olsen introduced *Fifty Cents* to Connecticut fifers.

Finnegan's Wake *Finnegan's* has been in the fife tradition as early as the 1930s, when it was collected in Connecticut by Acton Ostling and in Pennsylvania by Bayard. It is found in volume four of Howe's Musician's Omnibus (1864).

Fireman's Quickstep Another selection from AVF (1905); it is not the same tune as *Fireman's Reel*. In Connecticut, *The Jaybird* is played as a medley with *Fireman's Quickstep*. Ed Olsen relates this story from an elderly New York corpsman, Buck Johnston: The tune was played at firemen's dances in three strains. During the long tones of what is now the second strain, the audience was expected to yell "Fire! Fire! Fire!"

Frog in the Well Long part of the Moodus repertory as well as the old Yalesville corps, *Frog in the Well* was published in Hart's Instructor (1862).

Garry Owen was published as a fife tune c. 1808 in London, although it circulated in manuscript some years earlier. The title may be a corruption of Garryowen, an Irish town located in Limerick. In 1909, Columbia Records recorded *Garry Owen* as a medley with *The Campbells are Coming*. No documentation has emerged to support the legend that associates *Garry Owen* with Custer and the Battle of the Little Bighorn.

Girl I Left Behind Me Found occasionally in the 1790s and after 1814 with an alternate title, *Brighton Camp, Girl* is much more prevalent in the fife and drum literature of the 1800s. The tune *I Am Not Twenty*, published by Daniel Steele around 1815 may be the precursor of the version of *Girl* published in B & E (1862). By this time, the tune had become standard musical fare for troops departing from a city or camp. *Girl* did not lose its popularity with fifers once the Civil War was over. It is listed among 32 selections played by the Deep River Drum Corps c. 1900, 25-30 years before it was collected by Bayard from fifers in West Virginia and Pennsylvania.

Grandfather's Clock Published in 1876, Henry C. Work's famous song begins, "My grandfather's clock was too large for the shelf / So it stood ninety years on the floor." The tune was played by fife and drum corps long before it was collected in the Connecticut Valley by Ostling. The stick fencing is standard practice.

Granny Will Your Dog Bite appears in Winner's Primary School (1872) and AVF (1905).

Green Cockade Bayard believes that this tune was known in 1812 as a dance tune called *Sadler's Balloon*, a reference to James Sadler launched a balloon in 1784 and earned fame. As *Green Cockade*, this tune was memorialized by the Lancraft Drum corps who, according to Olsen, originated the singing part in the second strain.

Guidon appears in B & E (1862) on page 54 as *Quick Steps, For Drum Corps No. 1.* It is popular among reenactors as a streetbeat. For this book, Walt Sweet named it *The Guidon*.

Hell on the Wabash This tune is known to fifers primarily through B & E (1862).

Harum Scarum The earliest source I have found for this tune is the Fifer's Companion (1805). *Harum Scarum* is another revival whose current popularity is reinforced by the Carroll Collection and the Company books.

Hashup This drumbeat is attributed to Albert J. Frey, who played with the Enfield corps in 1923.

Huntington Although I met Colin Sterne at the 1992 Deep River Muster, it was Ed Olsen who told me the story of *Huntington*. Sterne wrote the tune (and Francis Goss the drumbeat) on the eve of a competition for the Union-Endicott Colonials in 1938. The U-E Colonials were founded in 1935 by Acton Ostling, who recruited members from the high school where he taught for many years. Sterne remembers Ostling as a "hard task-master," but he is known to most fifers and drummers as the compiler of Music of '76.

Inimitable was borrowed from fiddlers. Elias Howe published it in Ryan's Mammoth Collection (1883).

Irish Reel I have not found this tune anywhere other than in Connecticut Valley tradition. It is not the same *Irish Reel* that Bayard found in Pennsylvania in 1944, that tune being more like *Wind that Shakes the Barley*. The *Irish Reel* published here is most likely made up from fragments of older tunes. The 2nd strain is obviously borrowed from the 1747 dance tune, *Rakes of Mallow*.

Jaybird This selection from AVF (1905) evolved from a tune known as *Lady's Breastknot* c. 1775. The term "breastknot" refers to a ribbon bow used to decorate the bodices of ladies' gowns. How the tune acquired the *Jaybird* title is unknown. Bayard found nine versions of *Jaybird* circulating in western Pennsylvania beginning in 1930. The familiar music was used as an illustration in MacKinlay Kantor's novel, The Jaybird (1932). Kantor's story concerns a hobo who teaches his grandson to play the fife as they drift across the United States during the Great Depression. In 1976, "Sonny" Lions adapted the term "jaybird" to identify old-timers who no longer march or perform with the corps.

Jefferson and Liberty This tune emerged in the 1790s as *The Gobby-O*. It acquired the *Jefferson* title from a song-text which anticipated Republican success in the 1800 presidential election. Its seven verses welcomed the ousting of John Adams ("The Reign of Terror is no more") and forecast brilliant achievements by his hoped-for successor, Thomas Jefferson, "His Country's Glory, Home, and Stay." In the fife repertory, the tune has a long life which extends into the 1900s by means of the Company books. Both titles, *Gobby-O* and *Jefferson* follow the tune. In AVF (1905) it is called *Paul Revere's Ride*.

Just Before the Battle, Mother Written by George Root, and published in 1864, this sentimental Civil War song has a long drum corps history. With the drummers beating *Connecticut Halftime*, it was coupled with *Rakes of Limerick* and recorded in 1909 by the New York 12th Regiment Field Music as a medley for fife, drum and bugle (Columbia Records). Olsen recalls Lancraft using *Just Before the Battle* as a march-past for competitions in the 1940s.

Katy Hill A Valley tune as early as 1939, *Katy Hill* is a relatively obscure part of the fife and drum repertory. In the 1930s it was known by fifers in the Charles T. Kirk Corps from Brooklyn as *Haty Hill*, according to former Kirk fifer Ed Olsen.

Kingdom Coming This 1862 song is one of many written by Henry C. Work, a native of Middletown, Connecticut. Work wrote it in a dialect made popular by the minstrel groups that burlesqued the speech and deportment of the plantation slave. The text pokes fun at a plantation owner who fears the arrival of Yankee soldiers and the subsequent liberation of his slaves. An alternate title, *Jubilee*, is taken from the lyrics. *Kingdom Coming* circulated mostly in aural tradition in Connecticut and Pennsylvania where it acquired an alternate title, *The Doodletown Fifer*.

Lakes of Sligo This tune is known by several different titles including *Rocky Road to Dublin* and *I'm O'er Young to Marry Yet*. It was printed in Glasgow as *Loch Erroch Side* in Aird's third Selection (1788).

Marching through Georgia was written by Henry Clay Work in 1865. In some regions, this tune is incendiary.

Martin's Rattler This tune was written by William "Billy" Martin in 1904. Martin was drum major for the New York 12th Regiment Field Music in 1909 when they recorded for Columbia Records.

Minstrel Boy was first published in A Selection of Irish Melodies (London and Dublin: 1813). For this song, Sir John Stevenson set Thomas Moore's lyrics to an Irish melody called *Moreen*. -K.K.

Monumental Two-Four accompanies *Quick Step* on page 46 of B & E (1862).

Moon and Seven Stars appears in Rutherford's Collection (c.1756), in Aird's first Selection (1782), and in Hazeltine's Martial Music (1810). -K.K.

Nancy Hanks was President Lincoln's mother. The tune does not appear until 1905 (AVF).

New Tatter Jack This tune was printed as part of the afternoon duty in B & E (1862) and as *Tatter Jack* some years later in AVF (1905). The "Lanigan" tune collected by Bayard around 1940 seems to be more like *Bung Your Eye* than *Tatter Jack*, and a second tune, *Tatter Jack Walsh* again bears little resemblance to what we know as *Tatter Jack*. It is not clear if this tune is indeed a "new" version of an older *Tatter Jack*.

Northwest Passage This tune actually consists of one and a half tunes. It was revived by Ed Olsen, who heard *The Muckin' of Geordie's Byre* followed by *Shirt-Tail's Out, Wind's A-Blowin'* played in the movie, Northwest Passage (1940). He saw the movie several times in order to learn the tunes but could not remember the second half of *Shirt-Tails*, and so the incomplete medley was picked up by fife and drum corps as a single melody in three strains, *Northwest Passage*. In another instance, the two complete tunes were recorded as part of a longer medley, *Maryland My Maryland*, in 1908 by the Victor Drum, Fife, and Bugle Corps. *Muckin'* was printed in AVF (1905) as *O Lassie Art Thou Sleeping Yet* and circulated aurally in Connecticut as *Scotch Lassie* in the 1930s. During its long history it acquired still more titles: *Rainy Night, Sentry Box*, and *Brigade Quickstep*. The tune was published with the *Lassie* title in the 3rd volume of Riley's Flute Melodies (1820).

Old Dan Tucker As an old man, Dan Emmett claimed to have written this tune while still a teenager, naming it in honor of his dog, but according to S. Foster Damon "it seems to have made no impression until 1843, when it was first published." A minstrel "hit," the tune was quickly adopted by political songwriters as well as drum corps. For example, the abolitionist lyrics, "Get Off the Track!" were set to *Old Dan Tucker*. It was also the setting for a presidential campaign song, "Clay and Freylinghuysen"; the chorus began, "Hurrah! Hurrah! the Country's risin' / for Harry Clay and Freylinghuysen." *Dan Tucker* was played by the early Moodus corps.

Old Saybrook According to Ed Olsen, "Nobody knows where that came from; it's been kicking around for some time." It may have been the signature tune of the Old Saybrook corps, a group active c. 1900.

Oyster River appears in AVF (1905). The tune was part of the early repertory of the Fourth Degree Knights of Columbus Corps in Brooklyn during the 1930s.

Paddy on a Handcar Septimus Winner published *Paddy on the Handcar* in his Primary School for the Fife (1872) but not in his earlier Perfect Guide (1861). *Paddy* is similar to *Fifer's Masterpiece*, a tune that some believe may have been played by fifers during Shays' Rebellion (1787). I have found no evidence, such as a diary or tune-book entry, to support this claim, but *Fifer's Masterpiece* does turn up in the manuscript literature of the 1780-90s and in the printed literature in 1812 and 1815. It appears with no title in the handwritten collection c. 1778 of Thomas Nixon, a Massachusetts fifer.

Paddy O'Toole This tune was collected by Ostling in 1939 and 40 years later by the Company as *Paddy O'Toole*. It appears as *Land of Sweet Erin* in Kingsley's violin manuscript from Mansfield, Connecticut, c. 1795. O'Neill's contains this tune as *The Kinnegad Slashers, The Powers of Whiskey*, and *Bannocks of Barley Meal.*

Pet of the Pipers appears as *Doherty's Fancy* in O'Neill's Music of Ireland (1903). The 2nd strain is like *Come O'er the Stream, Charlie*. The tune was borrowed from fiddlers.

Powder Keg This drumbeat was played by the Chester Fife & Drum Corps. Ralph Sweet collected it without a title; for this book, Walt Sweet named it *The Powder Keg*.

Pig Town Fling Citing the modulation of the second part, Bayard states that this tune is of "fairly recent origin." He collected it from Pennsylvania fifers in 1929. However, *Pig Town Fling* is called *George Brown's Bon Vivant* in AVF (1905) and Elias Howe published it as *Kelton's Reel* in Ryan's Mammoth Collection (1883).

Plain Six-Eight is a general-purpose drumbeat. Compare it to *Fancy Six-Eight*.

Pumpkin Creek The tune was composed by Sanford E. ("Gus") Moeller; he also wrote a drumbeat (not shown). A prominent drummer and drum maker, Moeller was the instructor of the Charles W. Dickerson Field Music, founded as a Boy Scout corps in 1929. He taught them from 1933 until shortly before his death at age 82 in 1960.

Rally 'Round the Flag This song was written by George Root and published shortly after the Civil War began. Also known as *Battle-Cry of Freedom*, both titles were obtained from the opening lyrics, "Yes, we'll rally 'round the flag, boys, we'll rally once again / shouting the battle-cry of freedom." *Rally* is traditionally coupled with the drumbeat *Connecticut Halftime*.

Road to Boston The title of this remarkably stable tune probably refers to a song-text which is now lost. The tune, however, is preserved in three early Revolutionary War fife manuscripts. One of the versions follows the rhythm of a single-drag drumbeat. Other eighteenth-century musicians who were not fifers knew the tune as *Anson's Voyage* and *General Green's March*. A harmonized version of *Road* was printed in the Fifer's Companion (1805), and a drumbeat was written out in 1797 by Massachusetts drummer Benjamin Clark.

Sailor's Hornpipe appears as *Jack Henley's Maggot* in Johnson's Collection [c.1750]. A maggot is an odd notion; a whim. William William's fife manuscript of 1775 has this tune as a *Hornpipe*. In the 1760s, the title became *College Hornpipe*, changing to *Sailor's Hornpipe* in the 20th century. -K.K.

Scotty O'Neil was Bob McQuillen's first composition, published in Bob's Notebooks, Vol. I (1973). This talented dance musician continues to write and publish his music.

Sisters was known in the 1730s as a dance tune in 2/4 meter called *Buttered Peas*. *Peas* was the setting for several ballad opera songs; by the 1790s, it acquired another name, *Reel of Stumpie*, from lyrics which included, "Hap and row the feetie-o." At some point, the tune was cast into 6/8 meter.

The result was *Sisters,* a long-time drum corps favorite, collected independently by Bayard and Ostling in the 1930s.

Some Distance From Prussia, also called, *The Prussian*. The 1st strain appears in O'Neill's Music of Ireland (1903) as *The Pleasures of Home*. Maybe the word "*Prussia*" was mistaken for "*Pleasure.*" -W.D.S.

Star-Spangled Banner The first song to this tune was known as *The Anacreontic Song*, which was written in the 1770s and became the theme song for the meetings of a gentlemen's dinner club in London called the Anacreontic Society. The music, originally barred in 6/4, was by John Stafford Smith. The song soon became well known, both in England and America, and over 80 different and mostly patriotic poems were written to the tune between 1790 and 1820. Francis Scott Key's lyrics were written between September 13 and 17th, 1814. -K.K.

Steamboat Quickstep was published in Howe's Musician's Companion (1844).

Tallewan appears in AVF (1905).

Tearful Drummer appears in B & E (1862) on page 50 as *Funeral March No. 1*. For this book, Walt Sweet named it *The Tearful Drummer*.

Three Hundred Years Collected by Ostling as an untitled piece, he titled it *Three Hundred Years* in Music of '76. He chose the title whimsically, inspired by one town's anniversary celebration. The tune appears as *Lafayette's Arrival* in a manuscript tune collection which may represent selections from the post Civil War repertory of the Fifth Maryland Regiment.

Tramp! Tramp! Tramp! with music and words by Massachusetts-born composer and music educator George F. Root, this Civil-War popular song was published in sheet music in 1864 with the subtitle, *The Prisoners Hope*. -K.K.

Turkey in the Straw *Turkey* is the later title applied to a song which was published in 1834 as *Old Zip Coon*. The lyrics are in the dialect popularized by minstrel troupes, white performers who caricatured the appearance and habits of plantation slaves in their music and dance routines.

Village Quickstep appears in the Kingsley manuscript (c. 1795). The tune was played by the Moodus Drum and Fife Corps at a New York contest in 1879 and some fifty years later was still played in Connecticut. Bayard found that drummers in western Pennsylvania were playing a stick beat to it in 1944. In Howe's Musician's Companion (1844), the tune appears as *Bartlett's Quickstep*, with credit to Dr. John C. Bartlett of Chelmsford, Massachusetts.

Wearin' of the Green. This tune appears in The Spirit of the Nation (Dublin: 1845) to accompany *Up! For the Green*. Earlier, another set of lyrics bore the title, *The Wearing of the Green,* and told of an Irishman who had to leave his country because he wore green on his cape. -K.K.

Also the tune for the song, *The Rising of the Moon*.

When Johnny Comes Marching Home was written by Patrick S. Gilmore who published under the pseudonym Louis Lambert in 1863. Gilmore was a renowned conductor and cornet virtuoso. He was leader of the Salem (Massachusetts) Brass Band when he participated in a contest described in William White's History of Military Music (1944): "On December 15, 1856, the band performed at Mechanics Hall with Ned Kendall as bugle soloist. On this occasion, Kendall with his bugle and Gilmore on his cornet, played alternate strains of *Wood-Up Quickstep* and it was a difficult matter to tell which was superior." White goes on to describe John Holloway's *Wood-Up Quickstep* as the bugler's "ne plus ultra," much like a well-performed *Downfall of Paris* is regarded by fifers and drummers today.

Willie Weaver Published in Steele's Preceptor (1815), *Willie Weaver* has long been part of drum corps tradition. It was in the repertories of early corps including Moodus Drum and Fife Corps (1860), Deep River Drum Corps (1879), and Mattatuck Drum Band (1881). It was published in AFV (1905) as *Old Stop March*, most likely a reference to a now-lost drumbeat.

Wrecker's Daughter A song written in 1840 by Conrad Fay, *Wrecker's* was picked up by both brass bands and fife and drum corps. Arthur Schrader, former Music Associate at Old Sturbridge Village, defines a "wrecker" as someone who robs cargo from ships after luring them to shore by means of a false light. The subject of this song was a dangerous beauty who assisted her father in his illegal deeds. Bayard was surprised to find *Wrecker's Daughter* in the fiddle literature because he believed it to be a "standard fife tune, known to fifers everywhere." In 1879 the tune was played by the St. James corps during a drummer's convention held in Deep River. *Wrecker's* is printed in AVF (1905) and other fife books.

Yankee Doodle The origins of this familiar tune are obscured by the myths that have sprung up around it. It was heard in America as early as 1768, when a Boston newspaper reported "the Yankey doodle song" as the "capital piece" played by a newly-arriving British band of music. By the time of the Revolution, *Yankee Doodle* had become an American favorite, and nearly 100 years later fifers and drummers were still playing *Yankee Doodle*. When Army Inspector General Sylvester Churchill began drafting a new drill manual in 1858 he was told by his music consultant that "any drummer who has learned to beat the drum properly, will know at once" how to beat *Yankee Doodle*. It appears as a fifer's exercise in B & E (1862), but as duty repertoire in Gardiner Strube's Instructor (1869). Strube calls it *Double Time March #2* and dots the rhythm to match the single-drag drumbeat. In many versions, *Yankee Doodle* remains the signature tune of all traditional fife and drum corps. At Connecticut's 1888 drummers convention, it was one of the tunes played en masse by all the corps who attended. A New York newspaper called Moodus' performance of *Yankee Doodle* in 1879 their "pièce de résistance...the 'filling' brought out the greatest skill of the corps." The alternate version collected by Acton Ostling in 1939 is still played by Moodus, Chester, and other corps.

Yellow Rose of Texas was copyrighted in 1858 by Firth, Pond & Co., New York. The song was composed and arranged for the co-publisher, Charles H. Brown, of Jackson, Tennessee. Words and music were written by J. K., who remains unknown. -K.K.

York Fusiliers Thought to be British in origin, *York Fusiliers* was a favorite with American fifers of the late 1700s. It retained its *York* title in John Greenwood's collection of tunes for flute (1784) and in the Fifer's Companion (1805) but has a more American title of *The Congress* in both Aaron Thompson's fife manuscript (c. 1777-82) and in Willig's Compleat Tutor for the Fife (1805). A patriotic fifer, Thomas Nixon, called it *New York Fusiliers* when he wrote it into his tunebook around 1778. It appears that *York Fusiliers* has not survived from the 1700s; rather, it was revived, or re-introduced as a "new" piece into a body of music where many years before it had enjoyed some prominence. The cause was the bicentennial of the American Revolution, when so many fifers were looking for suitably "old" tunes to play at commemorations. *York Fusiliers* was never entirely lost. Bayard collected it in 1944 in Pennsylvania where fifers called it *Shenandoah*. An old-time fifer gave Bayard a description of the accompanying drumbeat. It differs considerably from George Carroll's drumbeat now popular.

Aird's Selection of Scotch, English, Irish, and Foreign Airs. vol. 1 [1782], vol. 3 [1788]. Reissue. Glasgow: J. McFadyen, [c.1800].

American Fife Instructor. N.p., n.p. 1888.

American Veteran Fifer (abbreviated as *AVF*). Cincinnati: Fillmore Music House, 1905. This book was complied from music contributed by veterans of the Civil War.

Ashworth, Charles Stewart. *A New, Useful and Complete System of Drum-beating.* Washington, D.C., 1812.

Bayard, Samuel P. *Dance to the Fiddle, March to the Fife.* University Park: Pennsylvania State University Press, 1982. Bayard began collecting in 1928. This comprehensive book shows the folk process at work.

Bruce, George B. and Daniel Decatur Emmett. *The Drummers' and Fifers' Guide* (abbreviated as *B & E*). New York: Firth, Pond & Co., 1862. Bruce was a drum major and band instructor in the U.S. Army. Emmett was not only an ex-army fifer, but also a fiddler, composer, and stage performer. In 1843, he founded the Virginia Minstrels and had a long career on the minstrel stage. Their book was intended as a self-instructor in rudiments and repertory for musicians called to serve in the Civil War.

Carroll, George P. *The Carroll Collection of Ancient Martial Musick.* 2 vols. N.p., [1960s].

Clark, Benjamin. *Benjamin Clark's Drum Book, 1797*, edited by Bob Castillo and Susan Cifaldi. [Sandy Hook:] The Hendrickson Group, 1989. This is a practical edition of Clark's handwritten collection of drum beats which is owned by the Massachusetts Historical Society.

The Company of Fifers and Drummers. Many tunes and drumbeats are included in their books:

The Company of Fifers & Drummers '76. [1974].

The Company of Fifers & Drummers Presents a Compendium of Medleys, Special Arrangements, Past Favorites. [1990].

Musical Selections for Fife and Drum. 2 vols. [1976].

The Compleat Tutor for the Fife. Philadelphia: George Willig, [c.1805].

Complete Instructions for the Fife. London: H. Andrews, [c.1808].

Damon, S. Foster. "A Series of Old American Songs." [A collection of broadside facsimiles and typed annotations now at Brown University.] 1936.

Ewen, David. *Popular American Composers from Revolutionary Times to Present.* New York: The H. W. Wilson Company, 1962.

The Fifer's Companion. Salem, Massachusetts: Joshua Cushing, [1805]. This is a truly American fife book, not a pirate of a London imprint. All the tunes are harmonized, even the camp duties. While some of these, such as **York Fusiliers**, have obvious British origins, others, including **Road to Boston**, seem to be distinctly American.

Fuld, James J. *The Book of World-Famous Music: Classical, Popular and Folk.* 3rd. ed. New York: Dover Publications, 1985.

Gibbs, Giles, Jr. [Manuscript collection of tunes for the fife.] Ellington, Connecticut, 1777. This handwritten collection is owned by the Connecticut Historical Society.

[Goulding] *New and Complete Instructions for the Fife.* London: G. Goulding, [c.1795].

Greenwood, John. [Manuscript collection of airs and dance melodies for German flute, 1784?] This handwritten collection is owned by the New-York Historical Society.

Hart, H. C. *Col. H. C. Hart's New and Improved Instructor for the Drum.* New York: 1862. Hart was a drum teacher who organized civilian and military "drum-bands" in Connecticut and New York. He published the *Instructor* in four separate issues during the 1860s.

Hazeltine, David. *Instructor in Martial Music.* Exeter, N.H.: C. Norris & Co. (1810).

Howe, Elias. [*Musician's Omnibus No. 4.*] Boston: Elias Howe, 1864.

___. *Second Part of The Musician's Companion.* Boston: Elias Howe, 1844.

Jackson, Richard, ed. *Popular Songs of Nineteenth-Century America.* New York: Dover Publications, 1976.

Johnson, J., *A Collection of Hornpipes,* book 2 (London: [c.1750], 4).

Kingsley, Luther. "Luther Kingsley's Property." Mansfield, Connecticut, 1795. This handwritten music collection is owned by the Mansfield Historical Society. A microfilm is at the Connecticut Historical Society.

Lawrence, Vera Brodsky. *Music for Patriots, Politicians, and Presidents.* New York: Macmillan Publishing Co., 1975.

Lovering, Levi. *The Drummer's Assistant.* Philadelphia: Bacon & Co., [1819].

Fifth Maryland Regiment. A photocopy of a manuscript collection of post-Civil War fife tunes; kept at the Company library.

McQuillen, Bob. *Bob's Notebook I.* Peterborough, New Hampshire, 1973.

Messer, Don. *Don Messer's Way Down East Fiddlin' Tunes.* Toronto: G.V. Thompson, 1948.

National Tune Index: Part I, Eighteenth-century Secular Music (Kate Van Winkle Keller and Carolyn Rabson, 1980) and *Part II, Early American Wind and Ceremonial Music, 1636-1836* (Raoul F. Camus, 1989) were published by University Music Editions of New York.

New and Complete Preceptor for the Fife. Albany: Daniel Steele, [c.1815].

Nixon, Thomas. "Thomas Nixon Junior his Fife Book." Danbury, Connecticut, and New York, [c.1778]. This handwritten music collection is owned by the Framingham [Massachusetts] Historical Society.

O'Neill, Francis. *O'Neill's Music of Ireland.* Chicago: Lyon and Healy, 1903.

Ostling, Acton E., Sr. *Music of '76 for Traditional Fife and Drum Corps.* New York: Remick Music Corporation, 1939. Ostling once drummed with the Chester [Connecticut] corps. This is a collection of Connecticut Valley favorites from the 1930s.

Ramsay, Samuel. [Orderly book containing 6 song lyrics in manuscript]. Fort Pitt, Pennsylvania, 1759. This handwritten book is owned by the Cumberland County Historical Society.

Riley's Flute Melodies. vol. 1. (1814). vol. 3. New York: E. Riley, [1820-1825].

Rutherford's Compleat Collection of 200 . . . Country Dances, vol. 1 (London: David Rutherford, c. 1756).

Ryan's Mammoth Collection 1050 Reels and Jigs. Boston: Elias Howe, 1883.

Shattuck, Abel. "A. Shattucks Book." [Massachusetts, c.1801]. A handwritten tune collection owned by the Library of Congress.

Spaeth, Sigmund. *Read 'Em And Weep: The Songs You Forgot To Remember*. New York: Doubleday Page & Company, 1927.

Strube, Gardiner A. *Strube's Drum and Fife Instructor*. New York: D. Appleton and Co., 1869. Strube's system of instruction was adopted April 17, 1869 by the War Department for the instruction of the Army and the Militia of the United States.

Sweet, Ralph. *The Fifer's Delight*. 5th edition. Enfield, Connecticut: Ralph Sweet, 1981.

Taylor, R. arr. *The Martial Music of Camp Dupont*. Philadelphia: G.E. Blake, [1816?].

Thompson, Aaron. "A Table of Time." New Jersey, 1777-1782. A handwritten tune collection owned by Yale University.

White, William C. *A History of Military Music in America*. New York: Exposition Press, 1944.

Williams, William. [Commonplace book of tunes for the fife] Pawtuxett [Rhode Island] 1775. Owned by the John Hay Library at Brown University.

Winner, Septimus. *Winner's Perfect Guide for the Fife*. Boston: Oliver Ditson and Co., 1861.

Winner, Septimus. *Winner's Primary School for the Fife*. Boston: Ditson and Co., 1872.

Index to Music

Italic titles and ⇨ lead to a contemporary title that is discussed on pp. 91 thru 98

CONTINUED NEXT PAGE

WINDSOR LOCKS, CONN
8
Conn. Regiment
Warehouse Point
The
End

Printed in Great Britain
by Amazon

64020229R00063